Love *in* Anime World

A hand-drawn coloring book

Queenie Wong

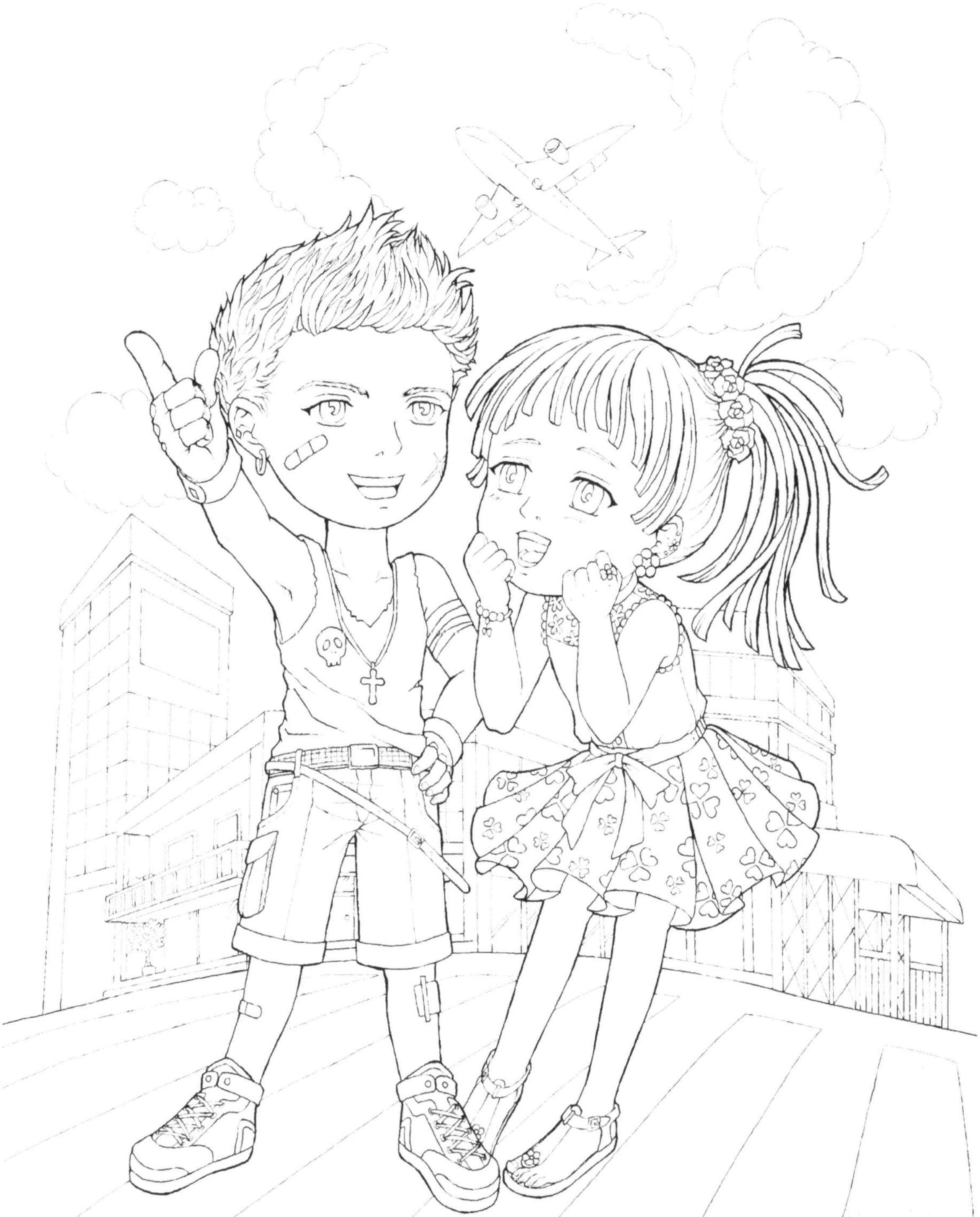

ISBN-13: 978-1546461999
ISBN-10: 154646199X
First published in United States in 2017
Illustrations by Queenie Wong
Wonger0050@yahoo.com.hk

This book is drawn in anime style. There are 30 pictures which includes below:

Close-up beauties: The first 5 pictures are good for coloring a make-up with details, such as blending colors for eye shadow, brushing the cheeks and putting lipsticks with shines.

Little sweety girls: The following 7 pictures are showing the full body of little girls in different dressing styles. Just to make how cute they could be.

Young ladies: The following 6 pictures are showing fashionable ladies in their unique characteristics.

Best friends: The following 5 pictures are showing 2 best friends having good time together.

Puppy Lovers: The last 7 pictures are narratively showing the interaction of a boy and a girl.

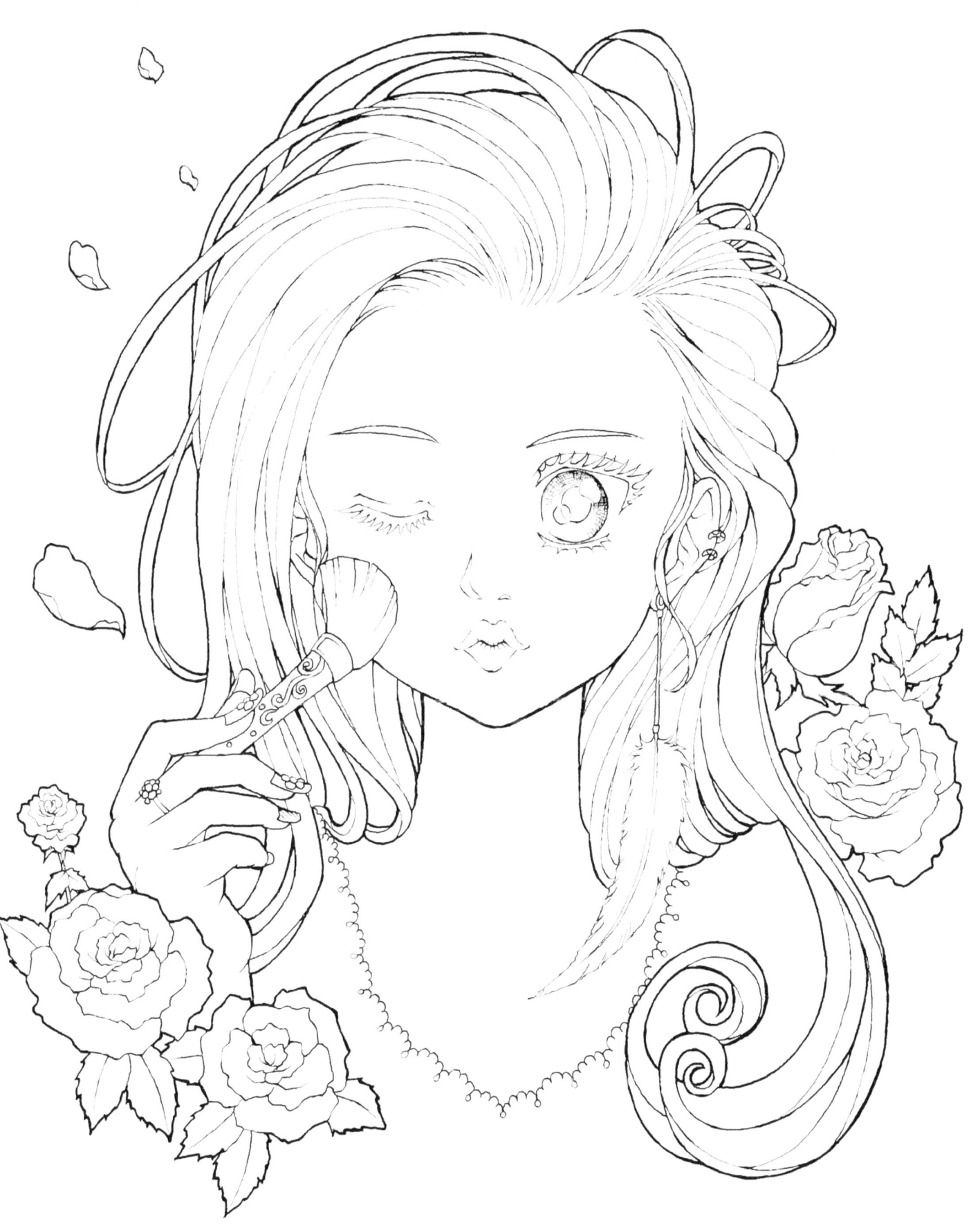

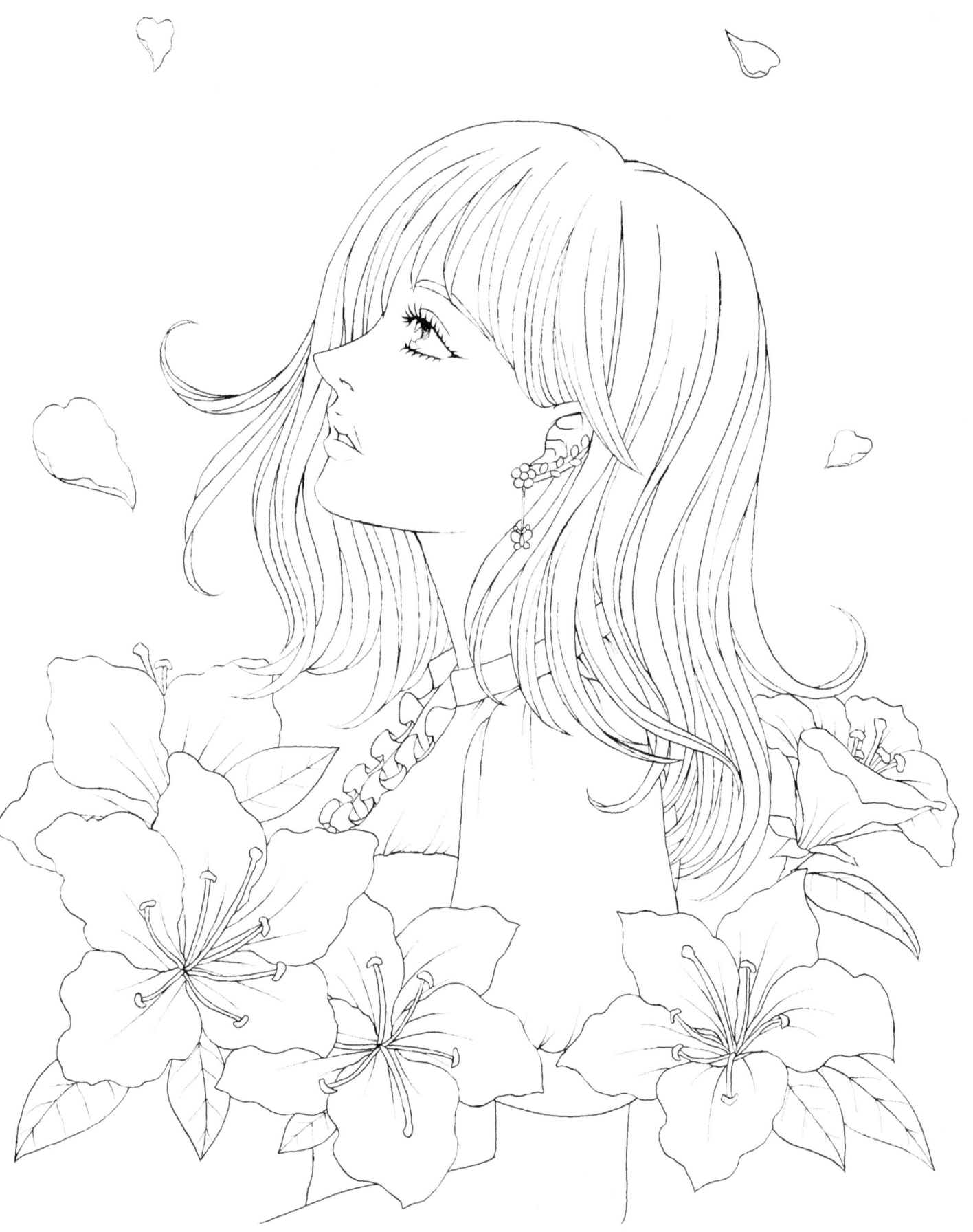

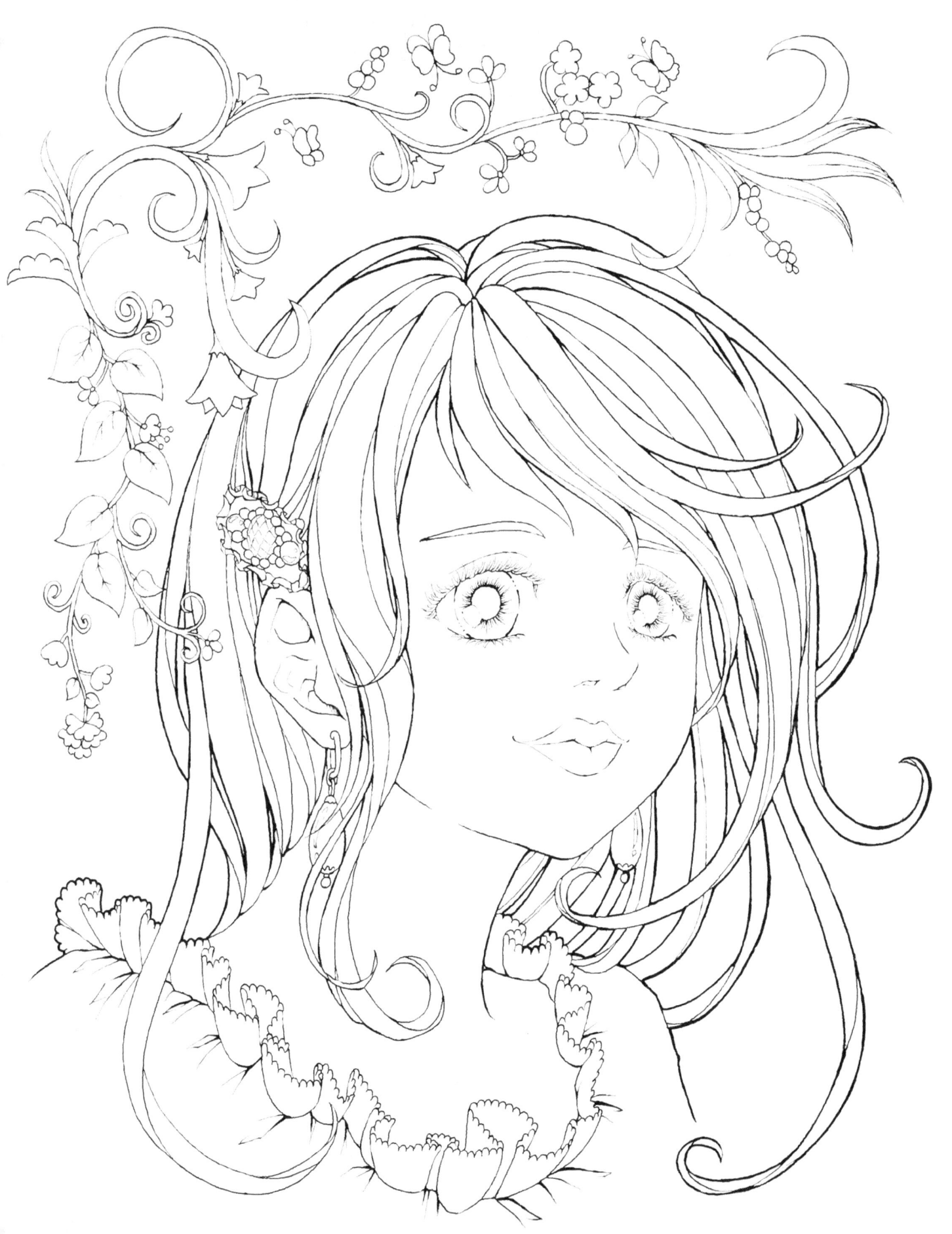

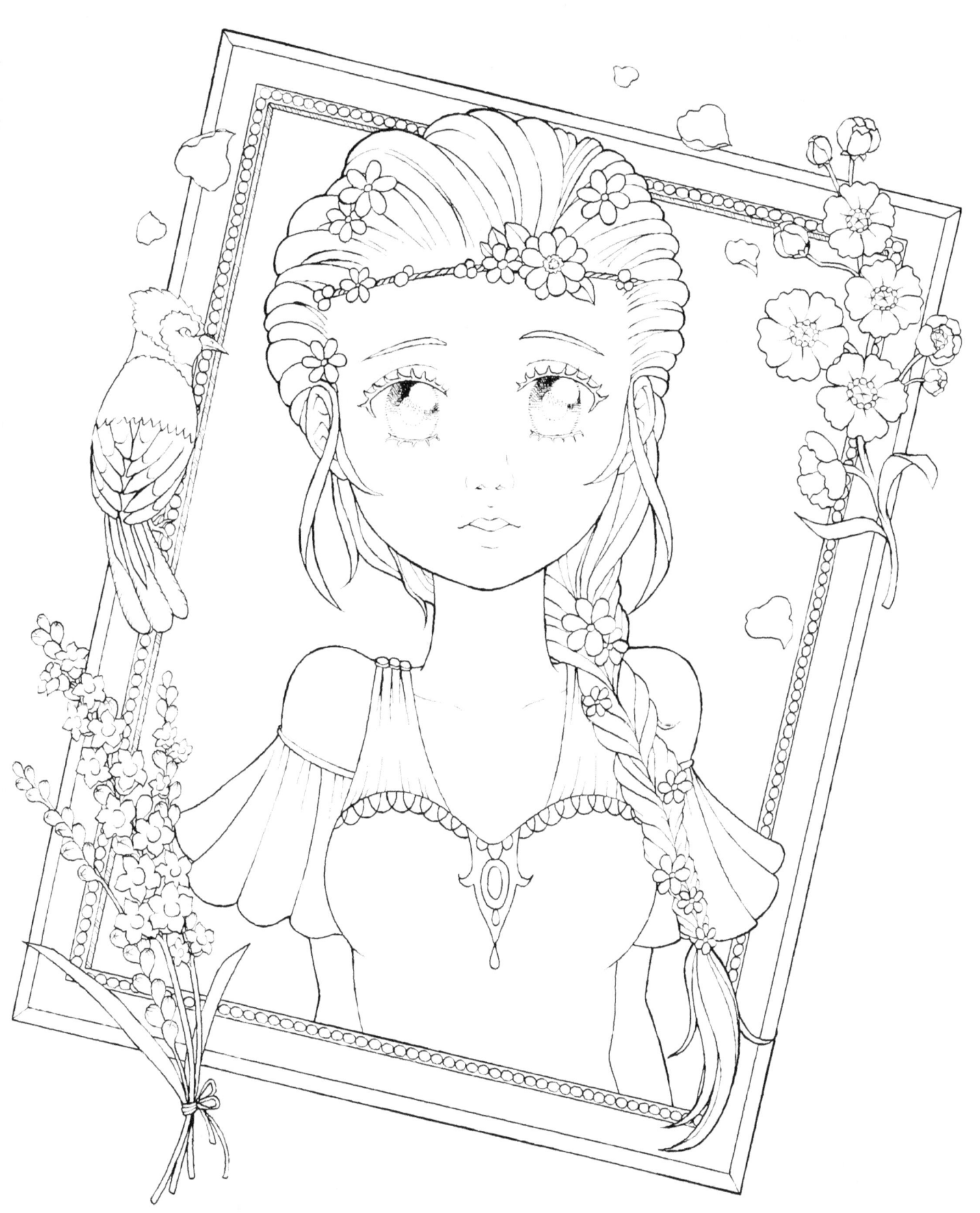

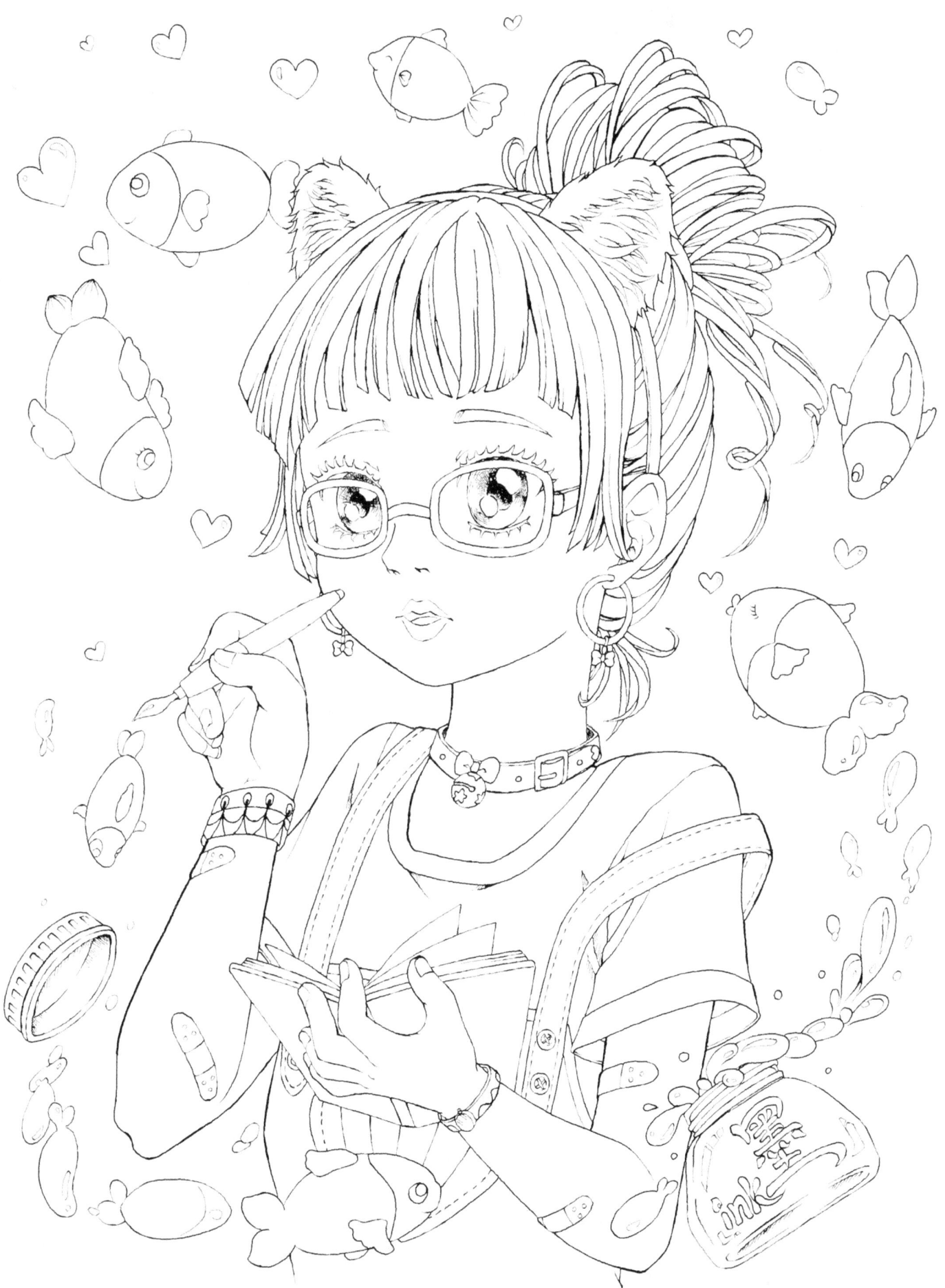

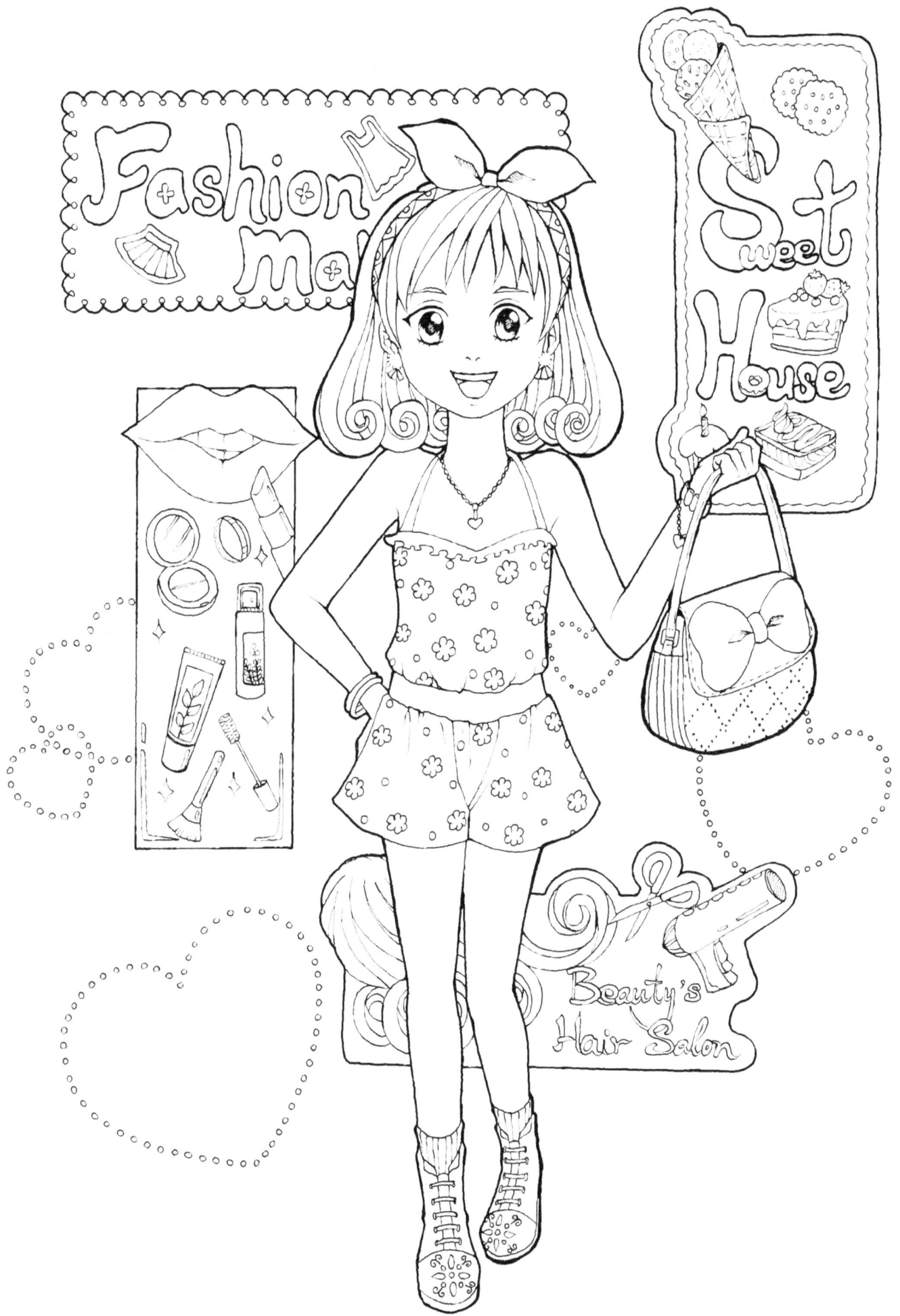

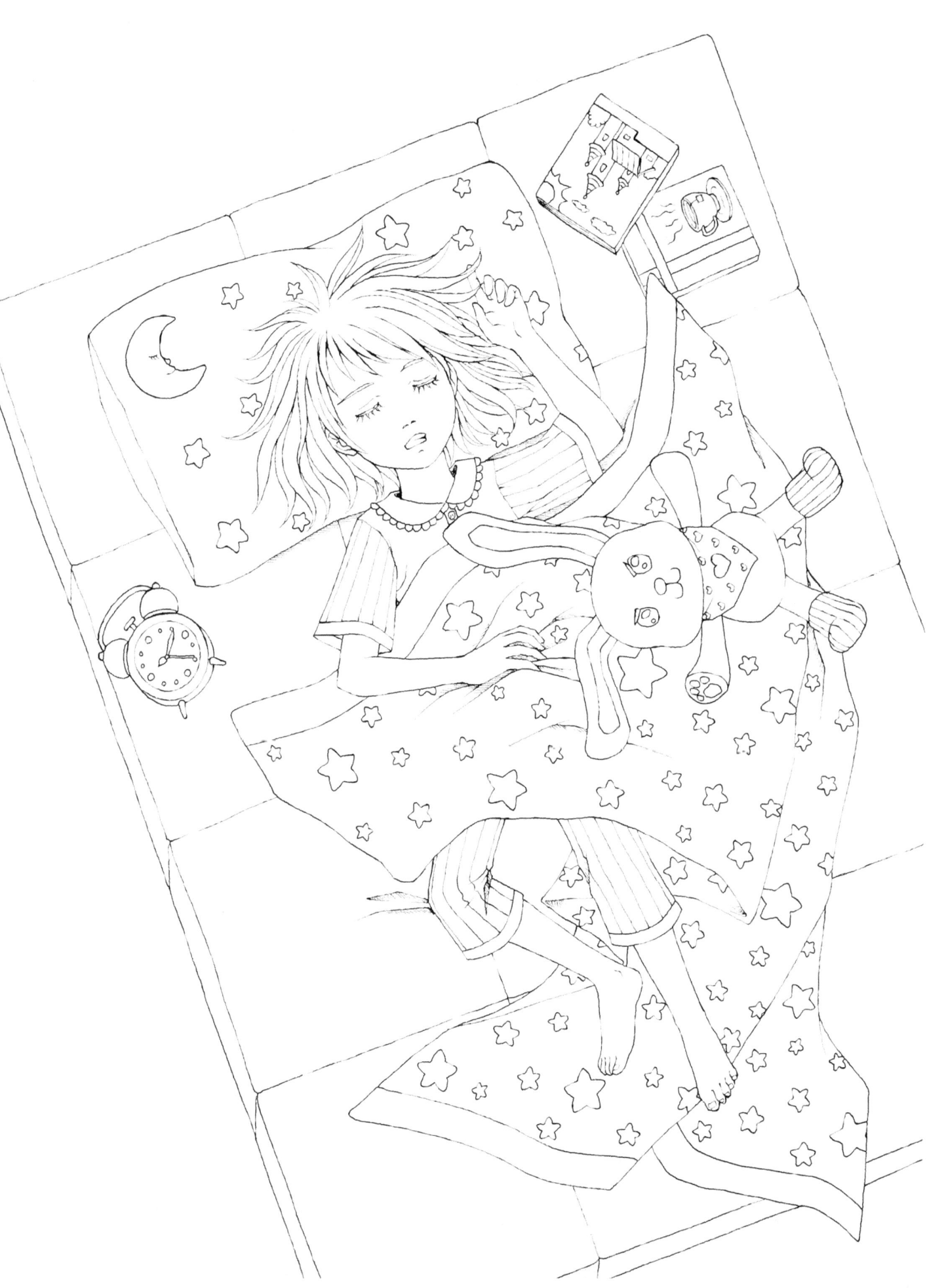

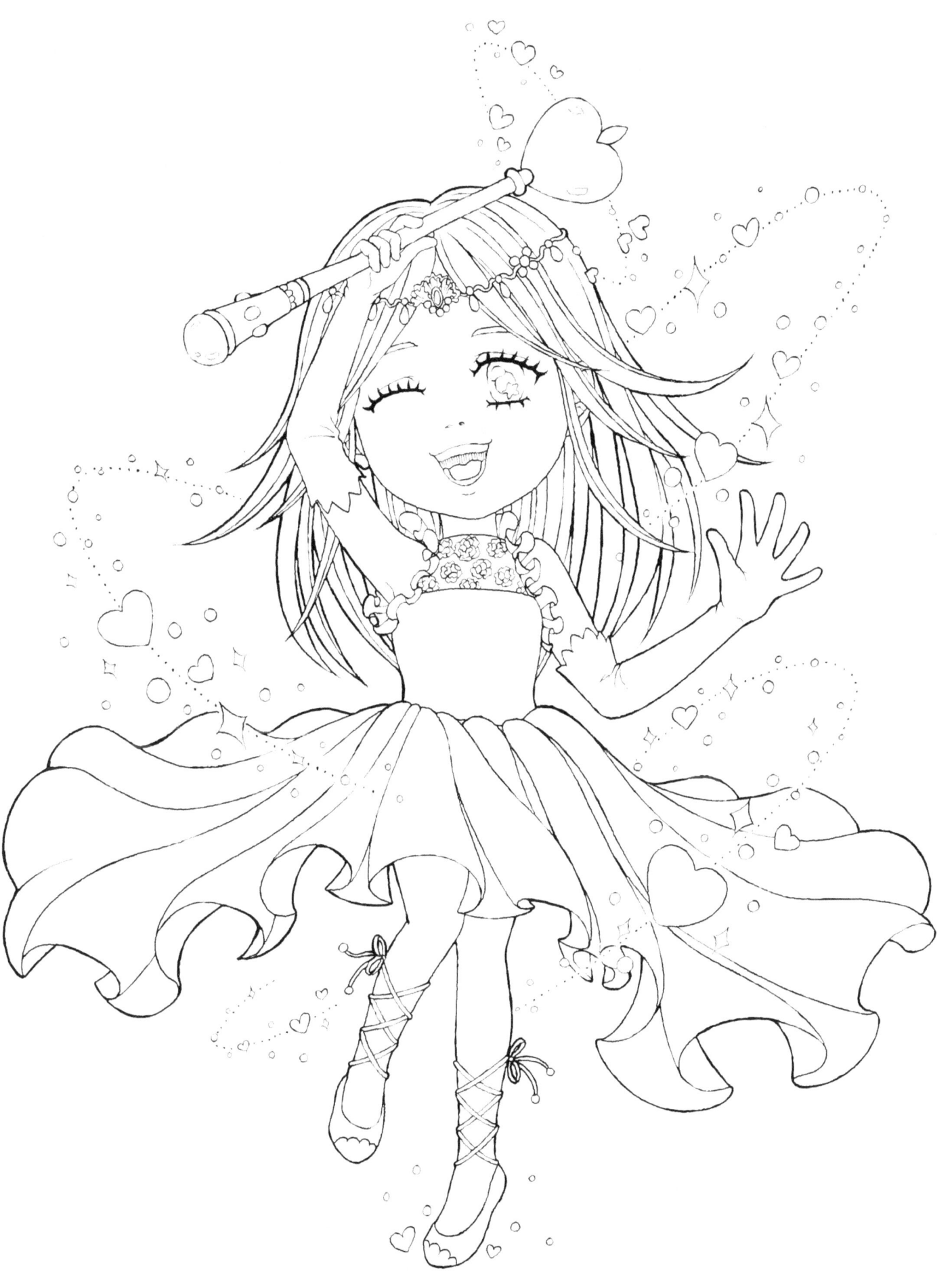

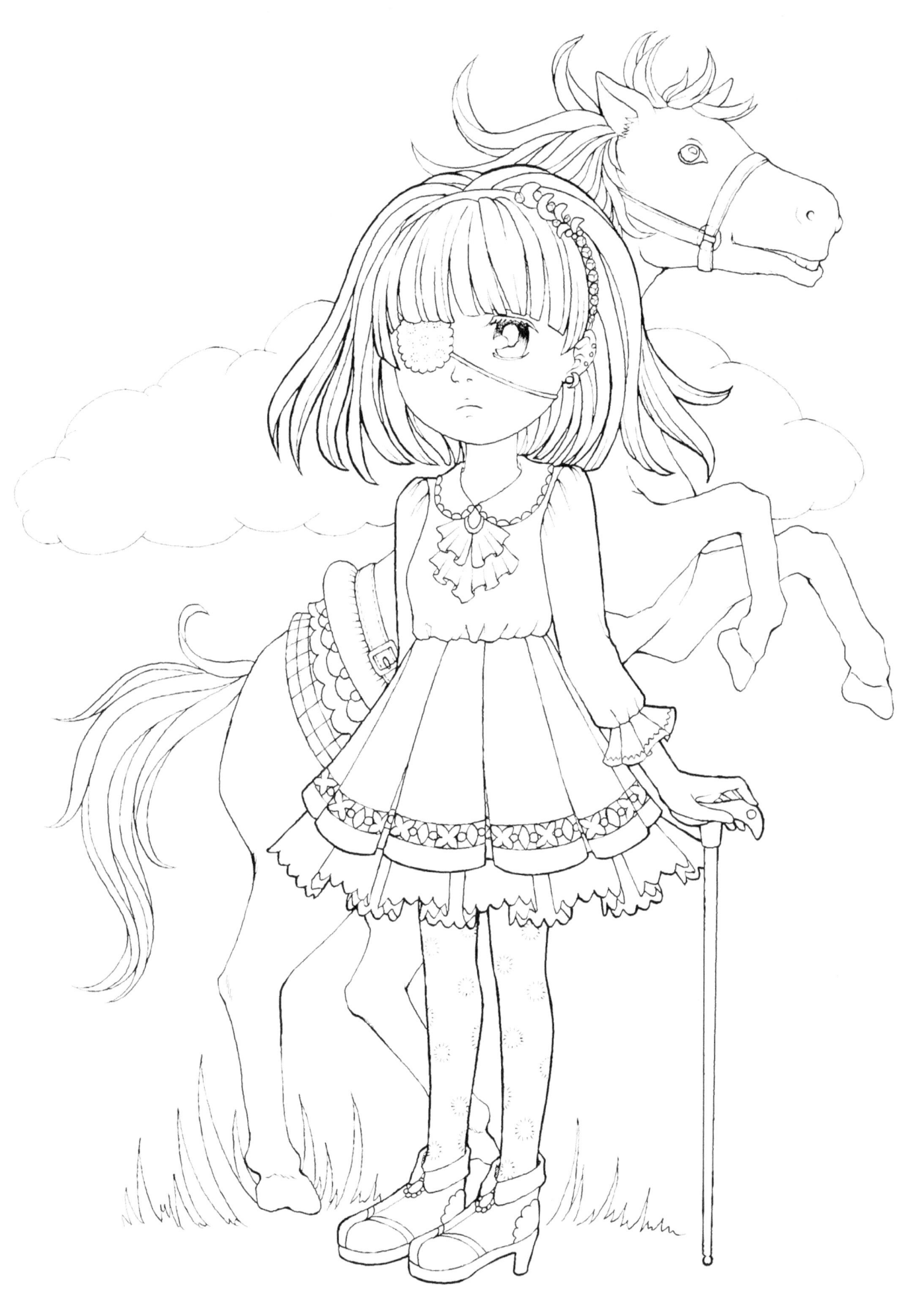

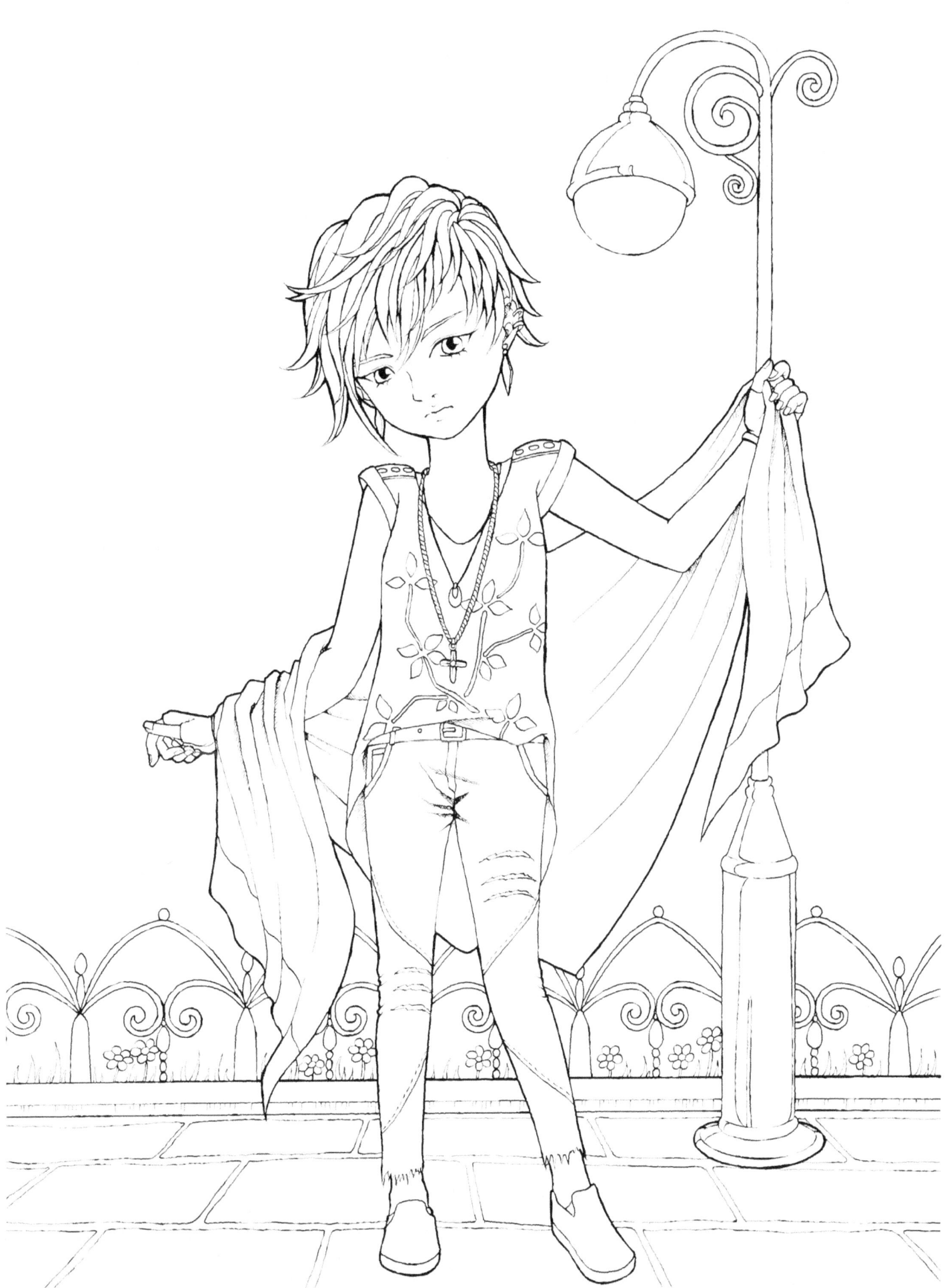

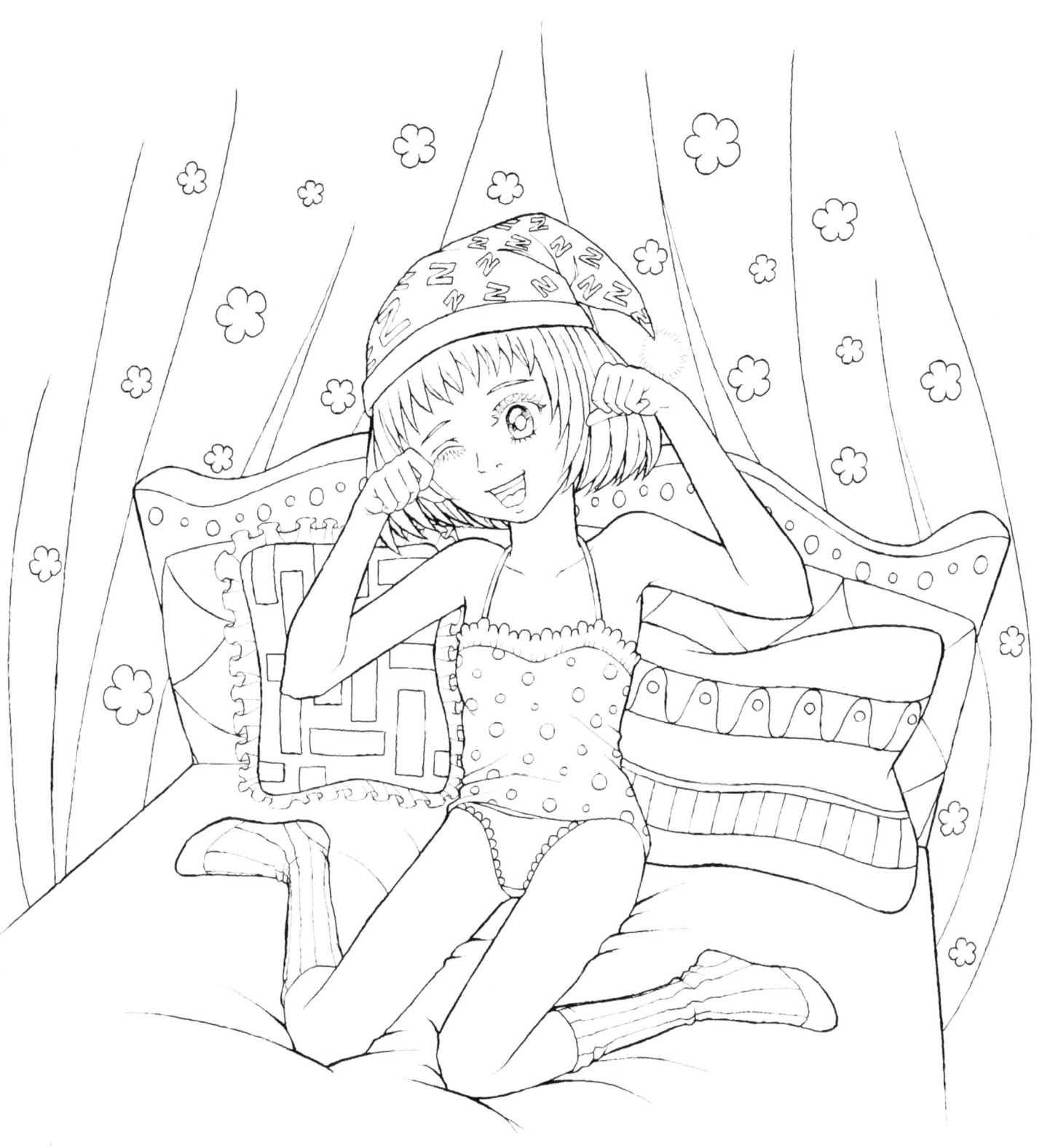

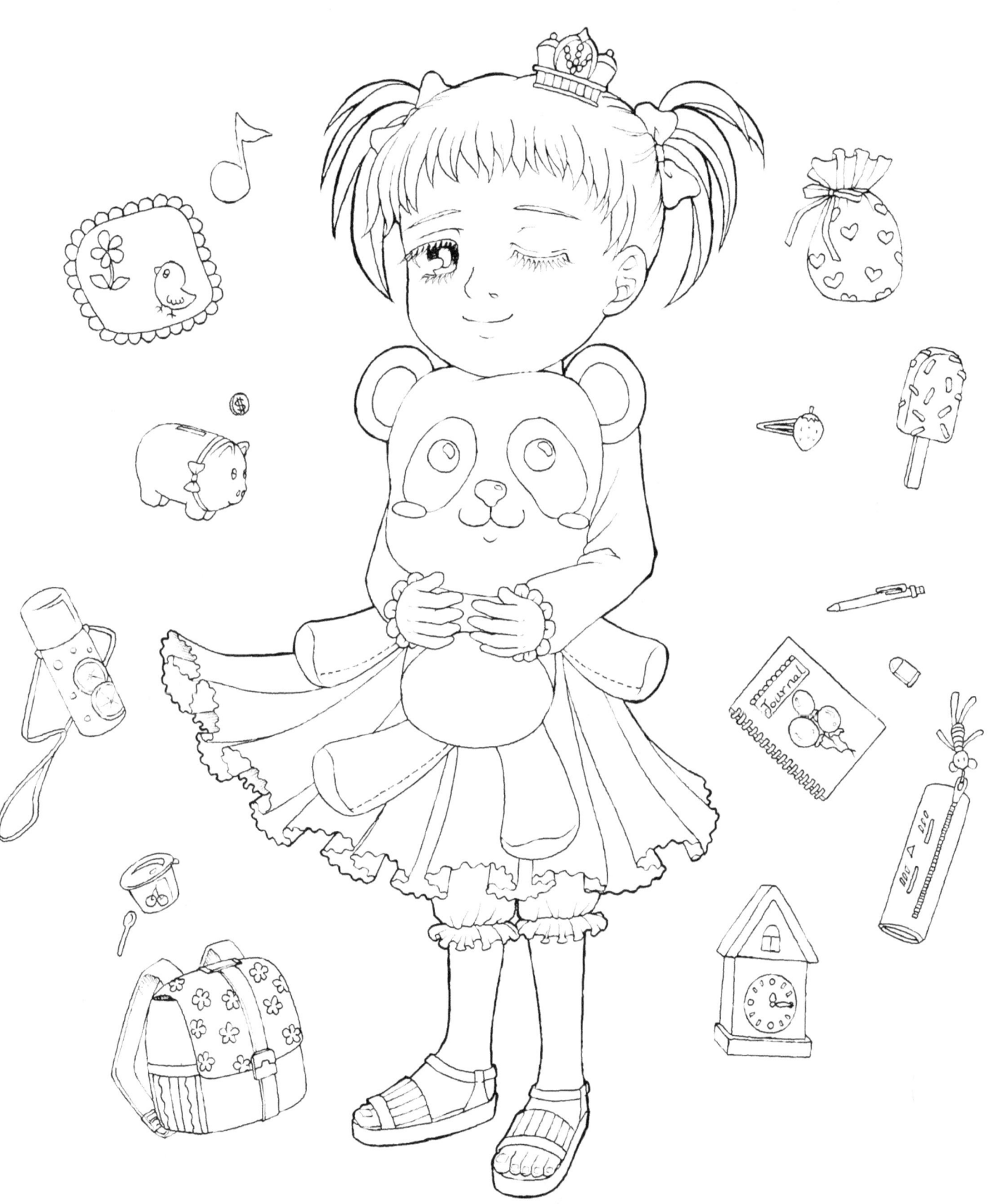

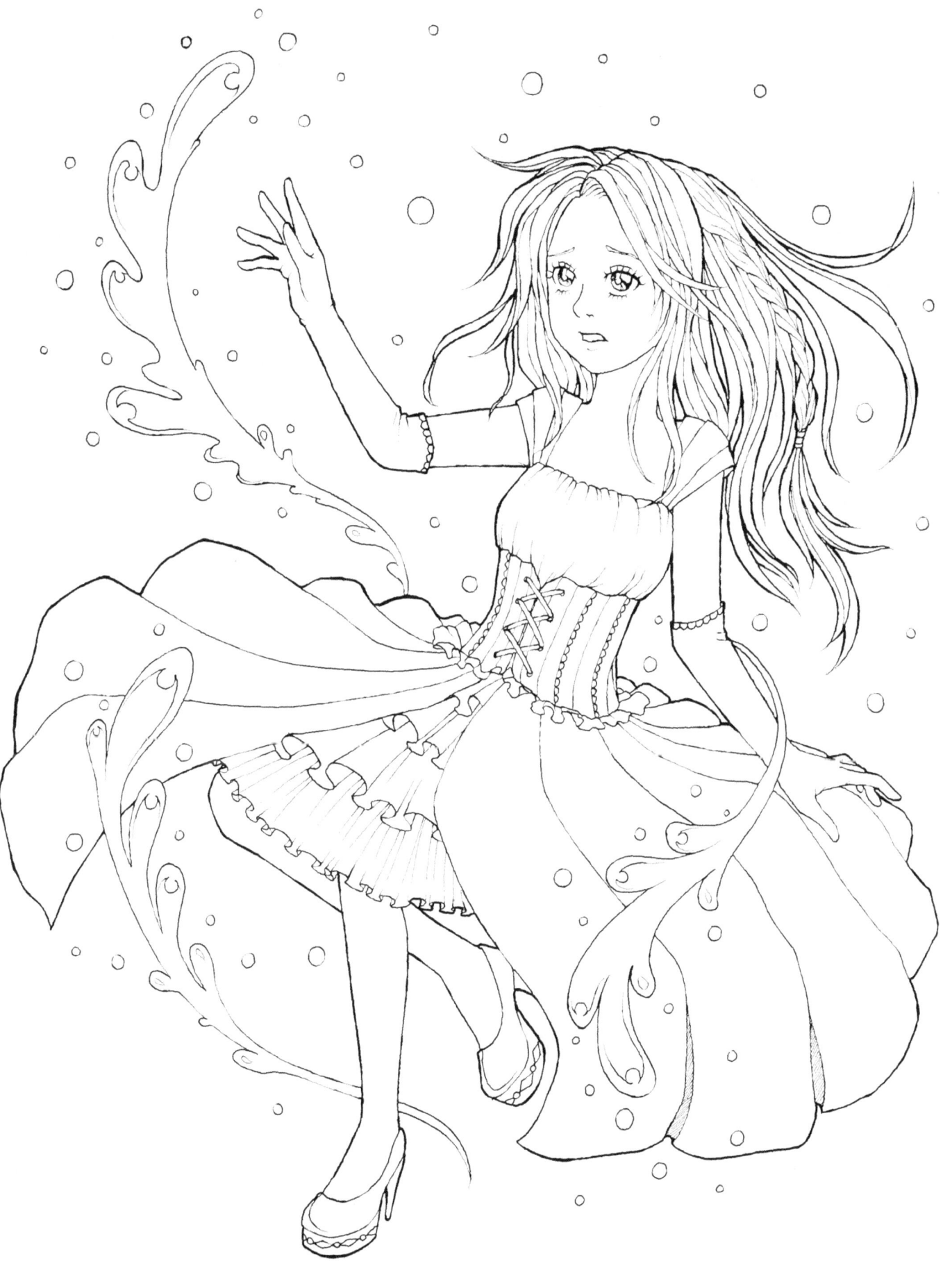

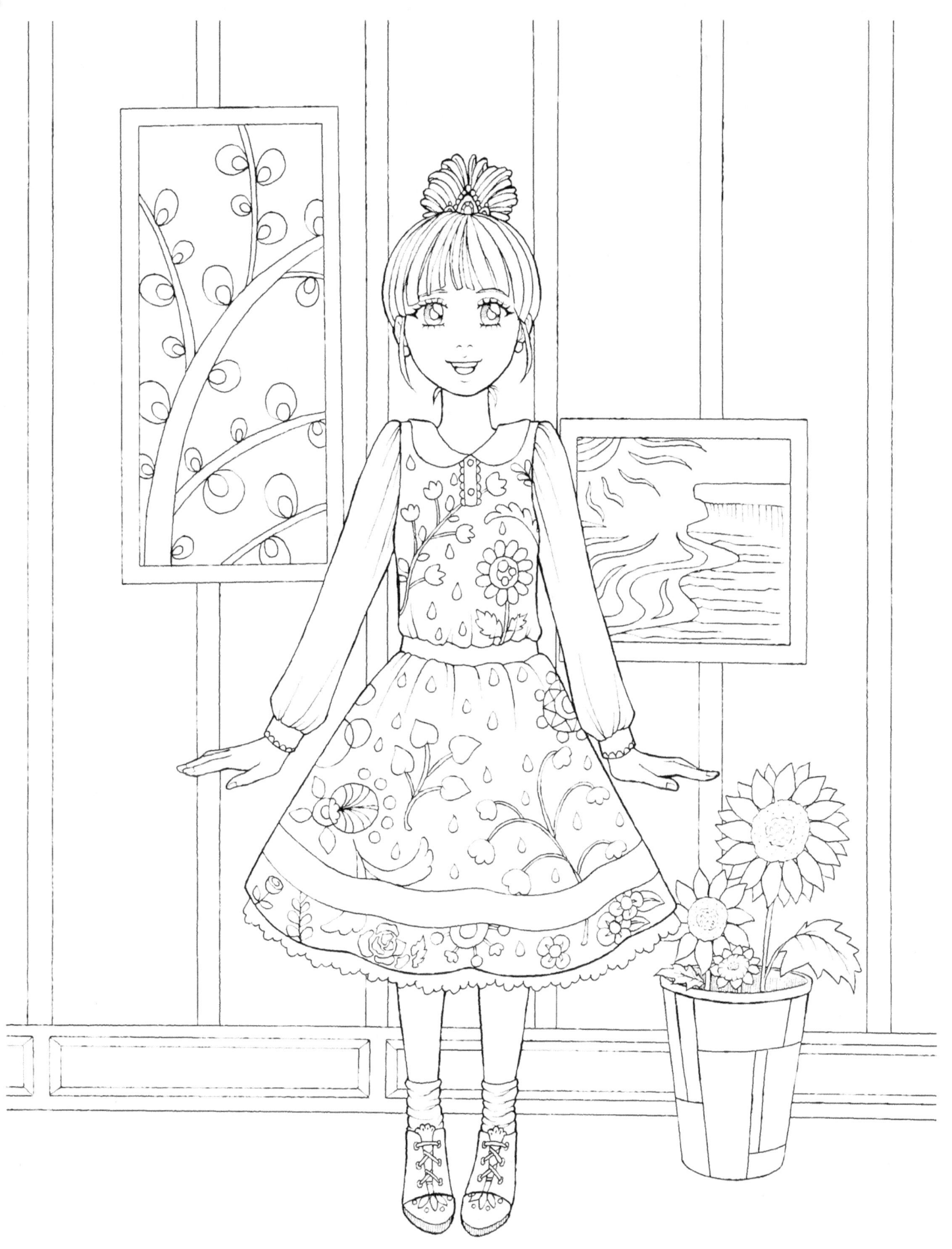

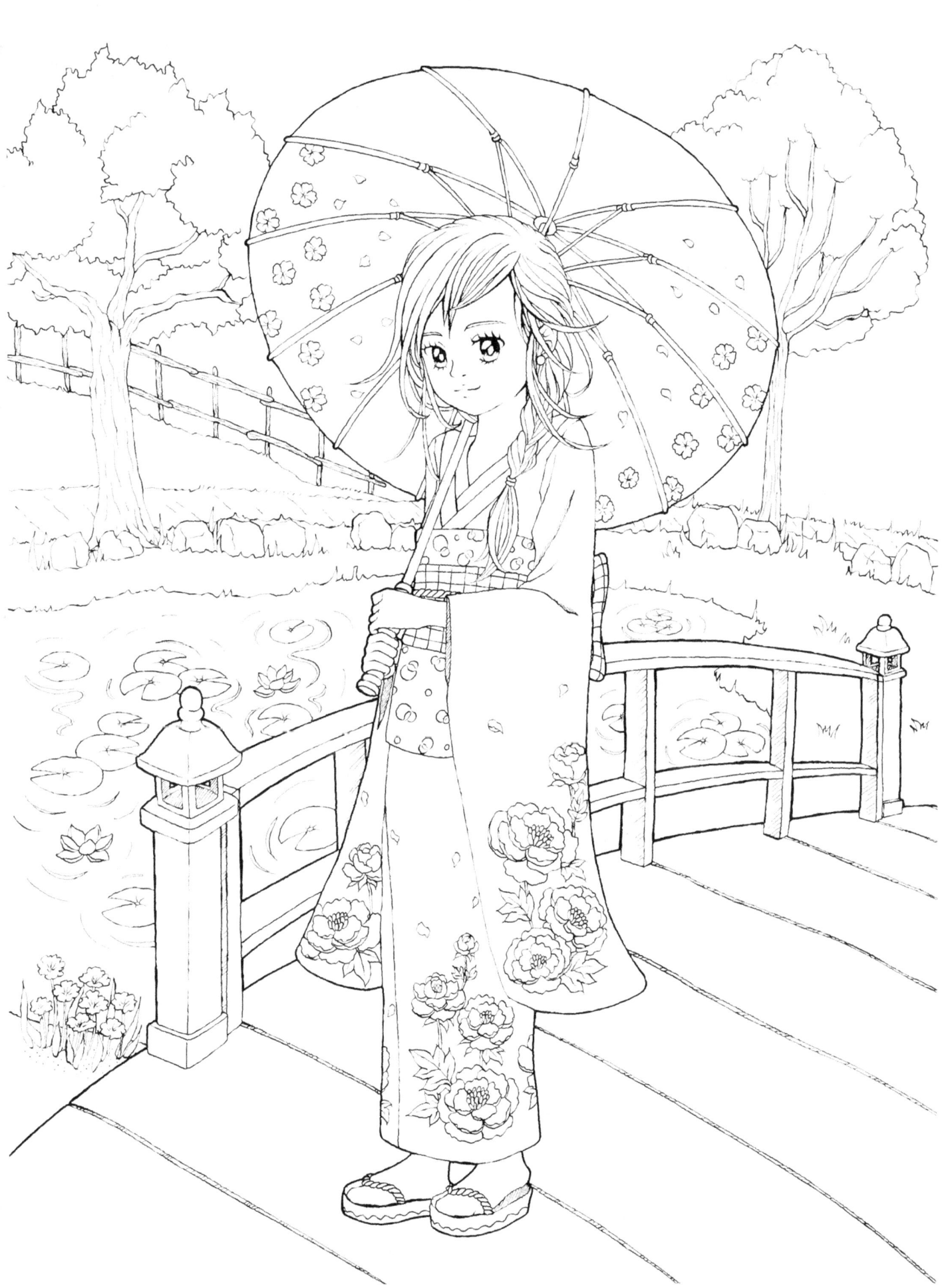

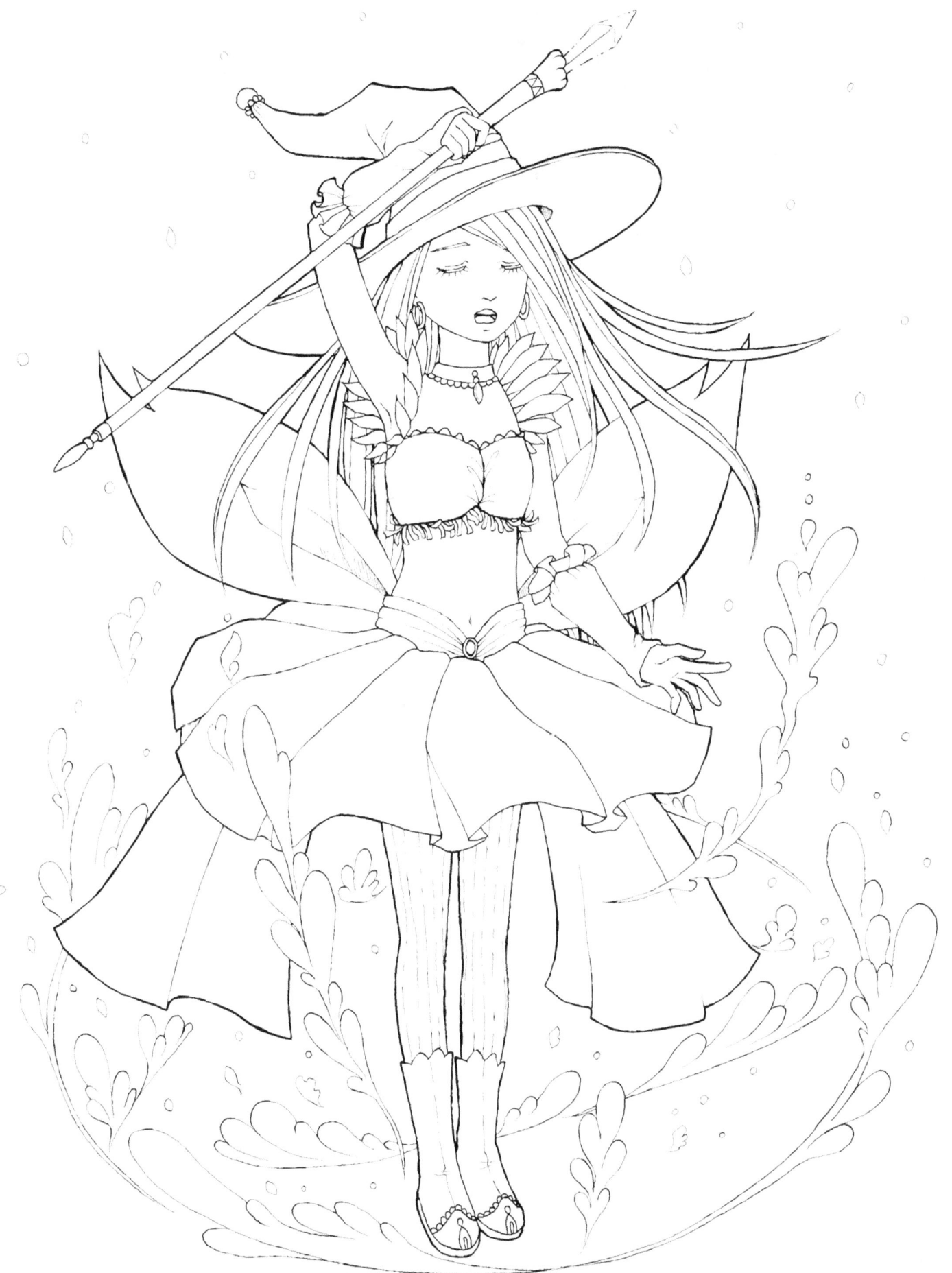

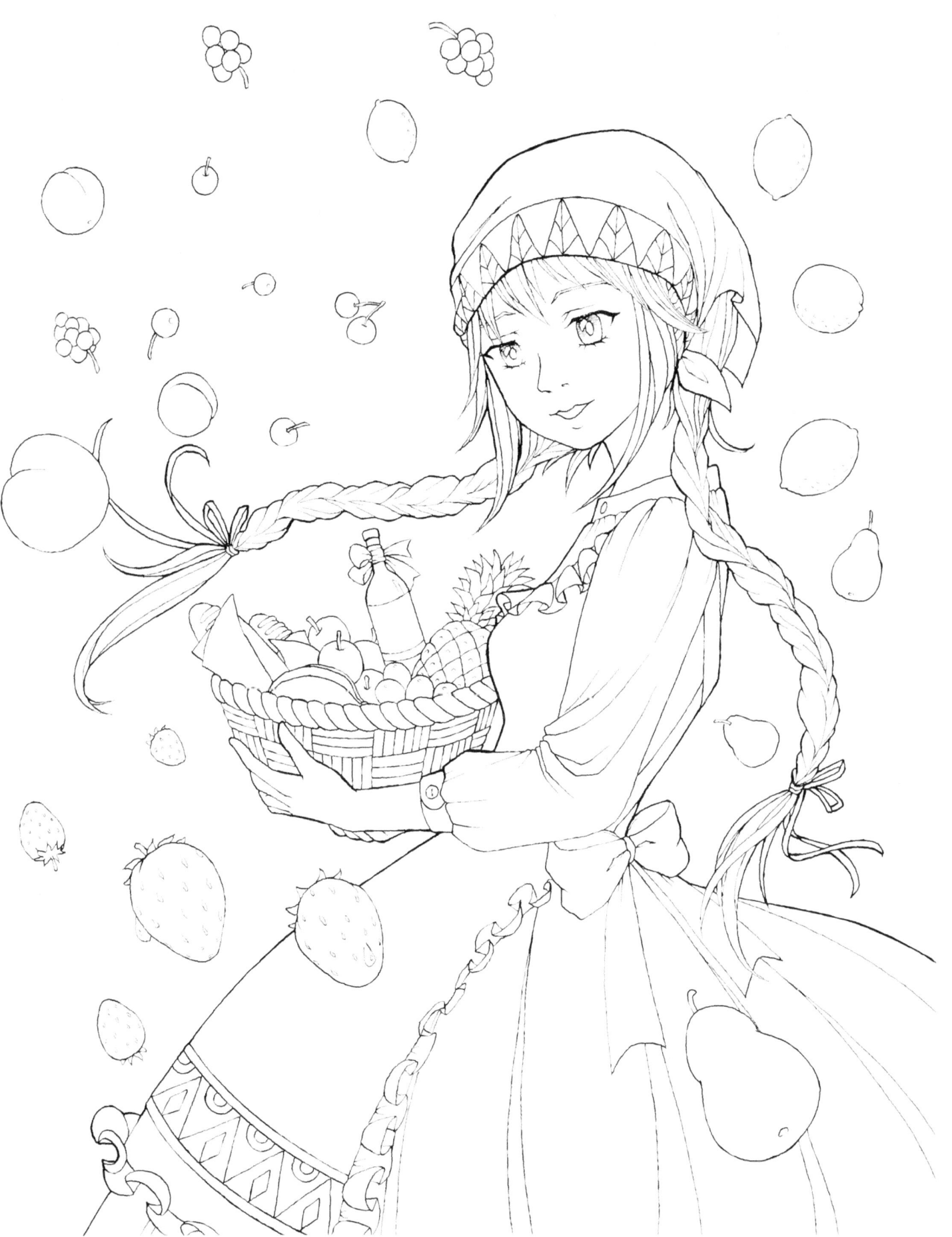

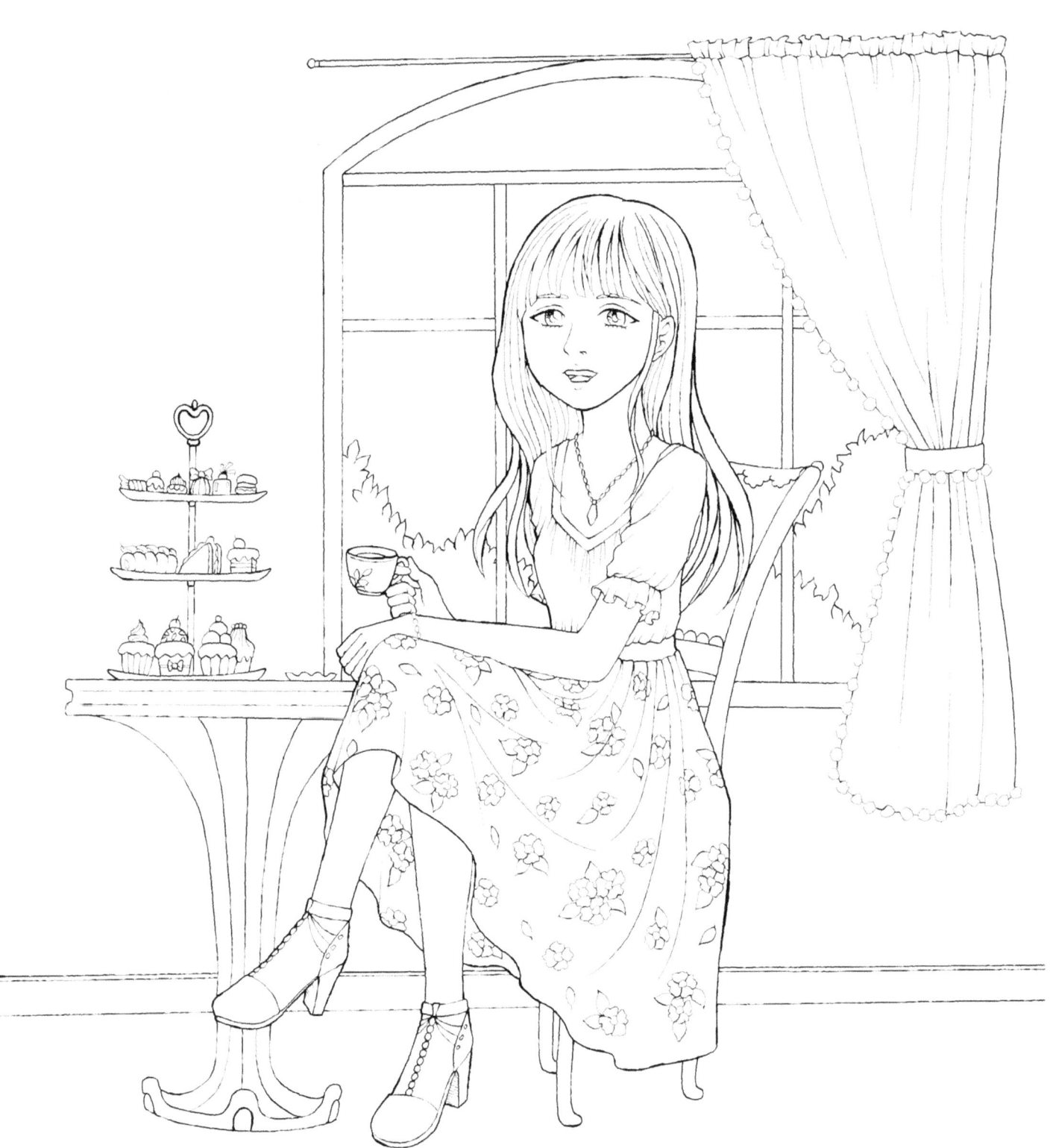

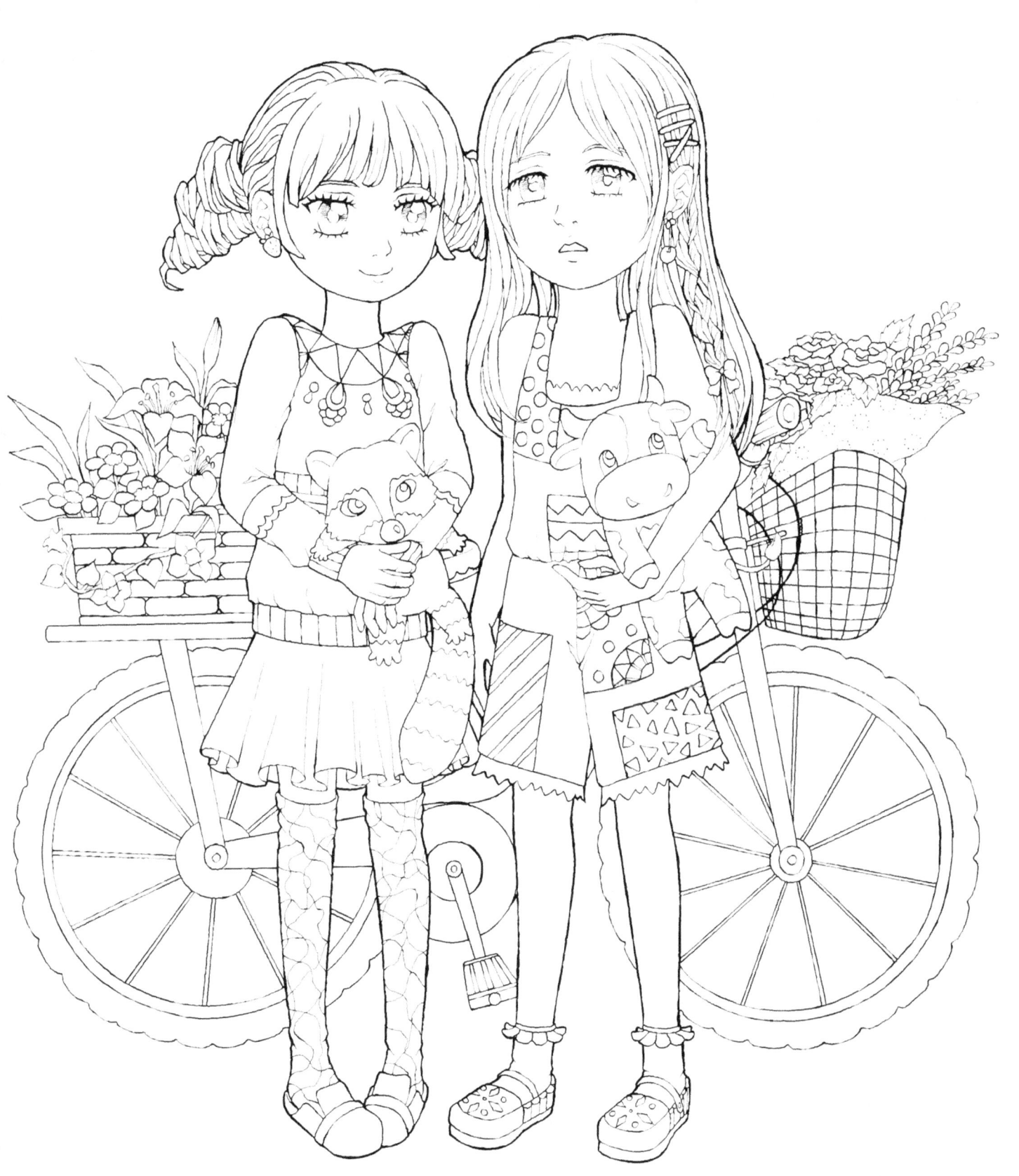

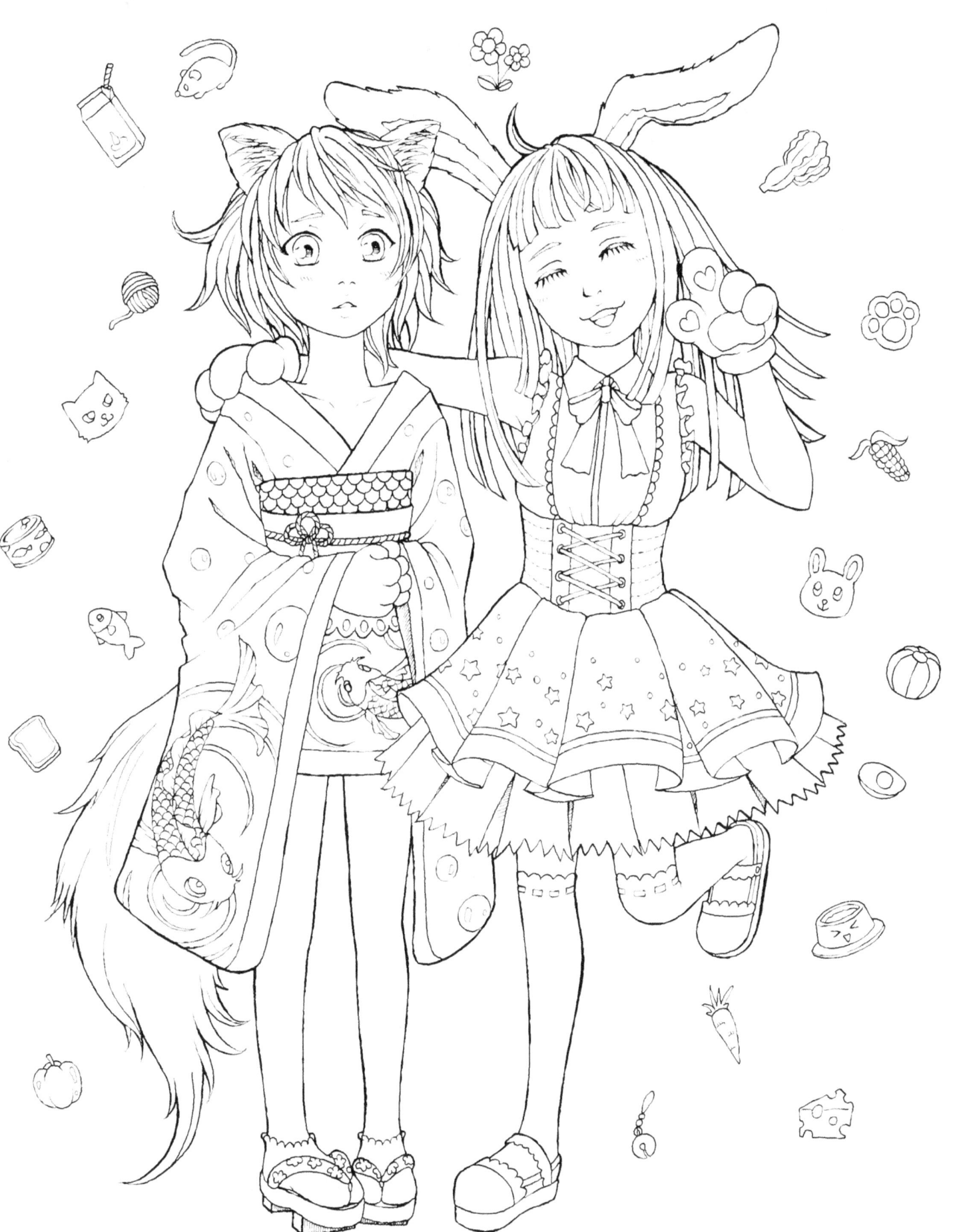

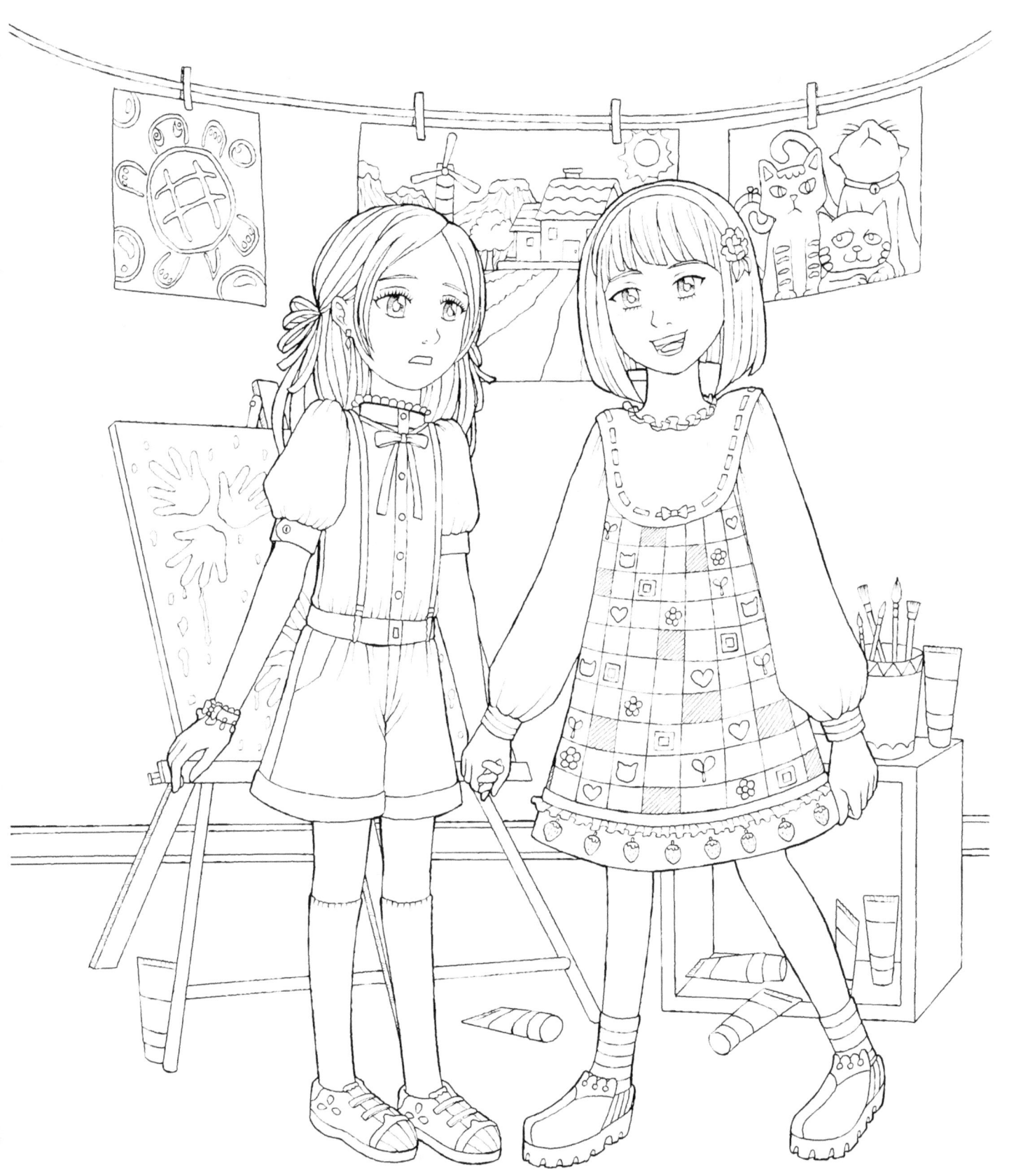

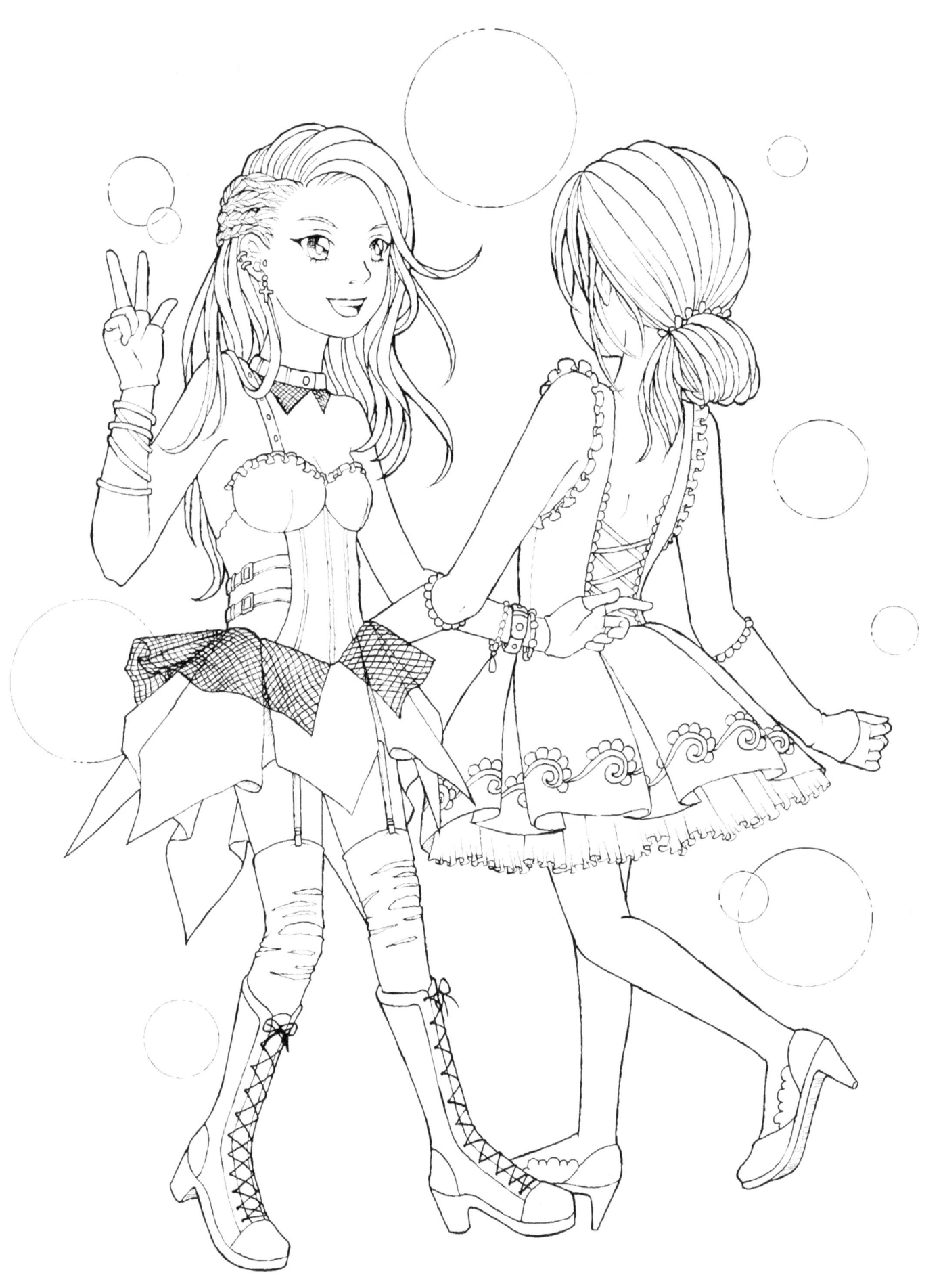

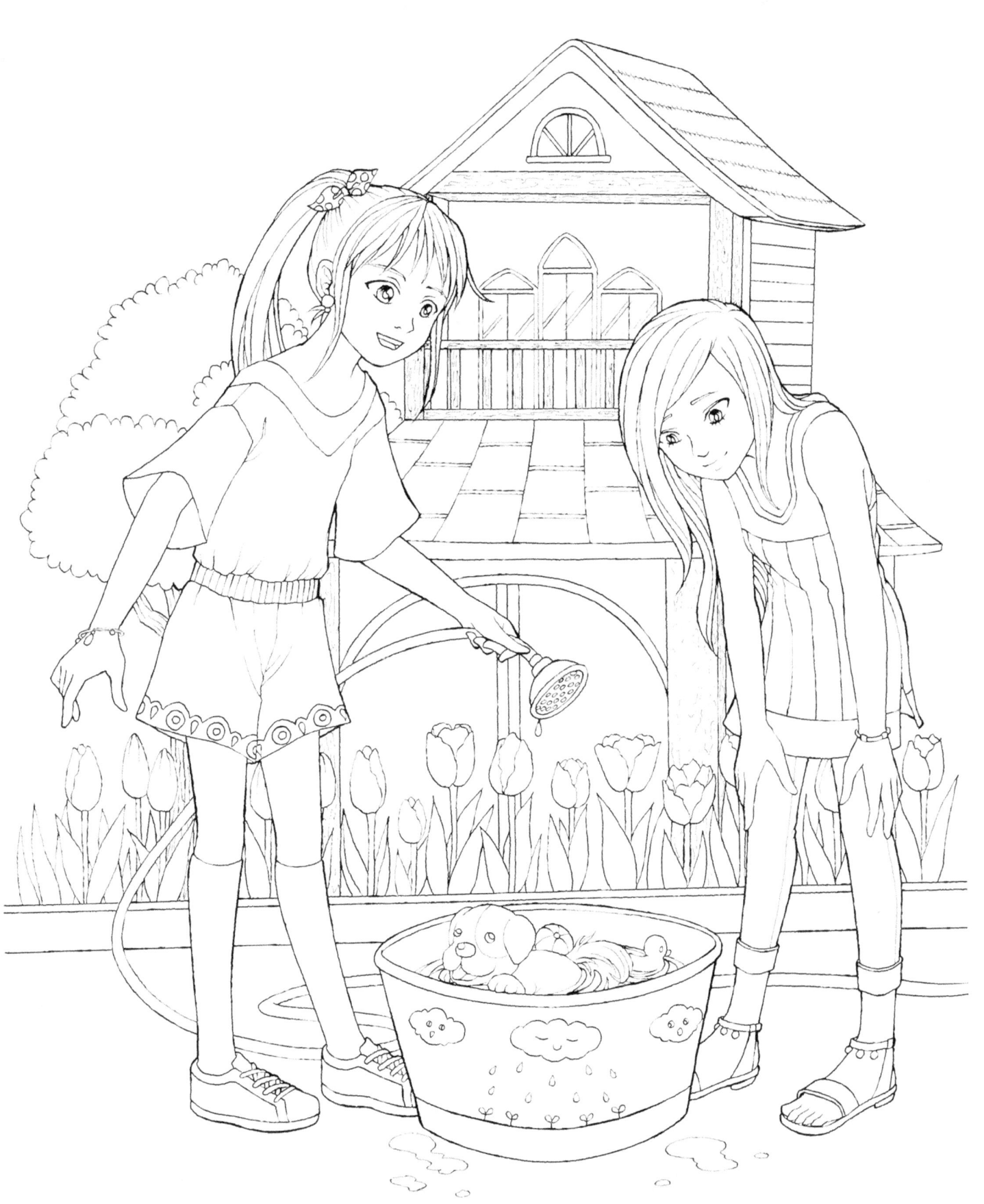

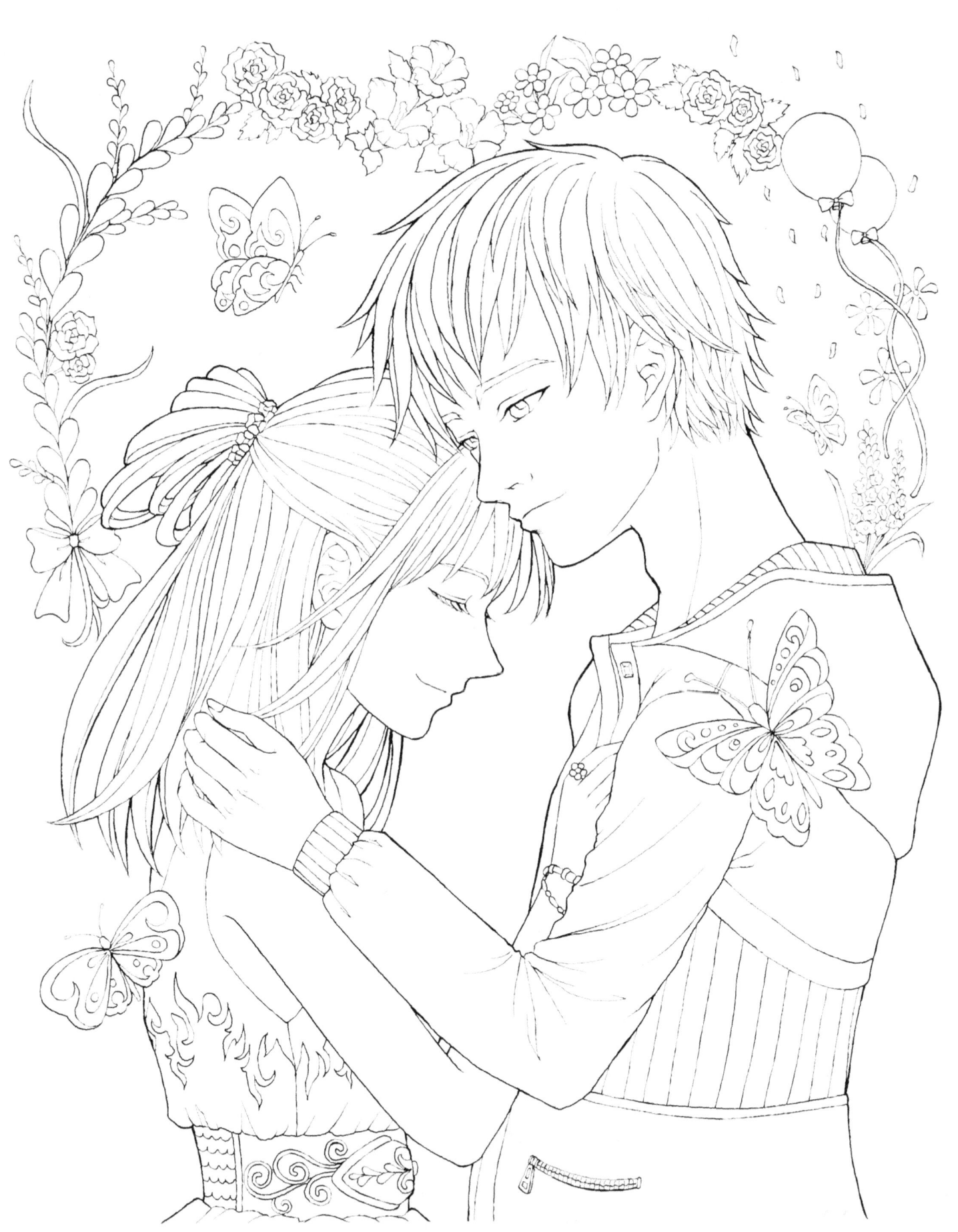

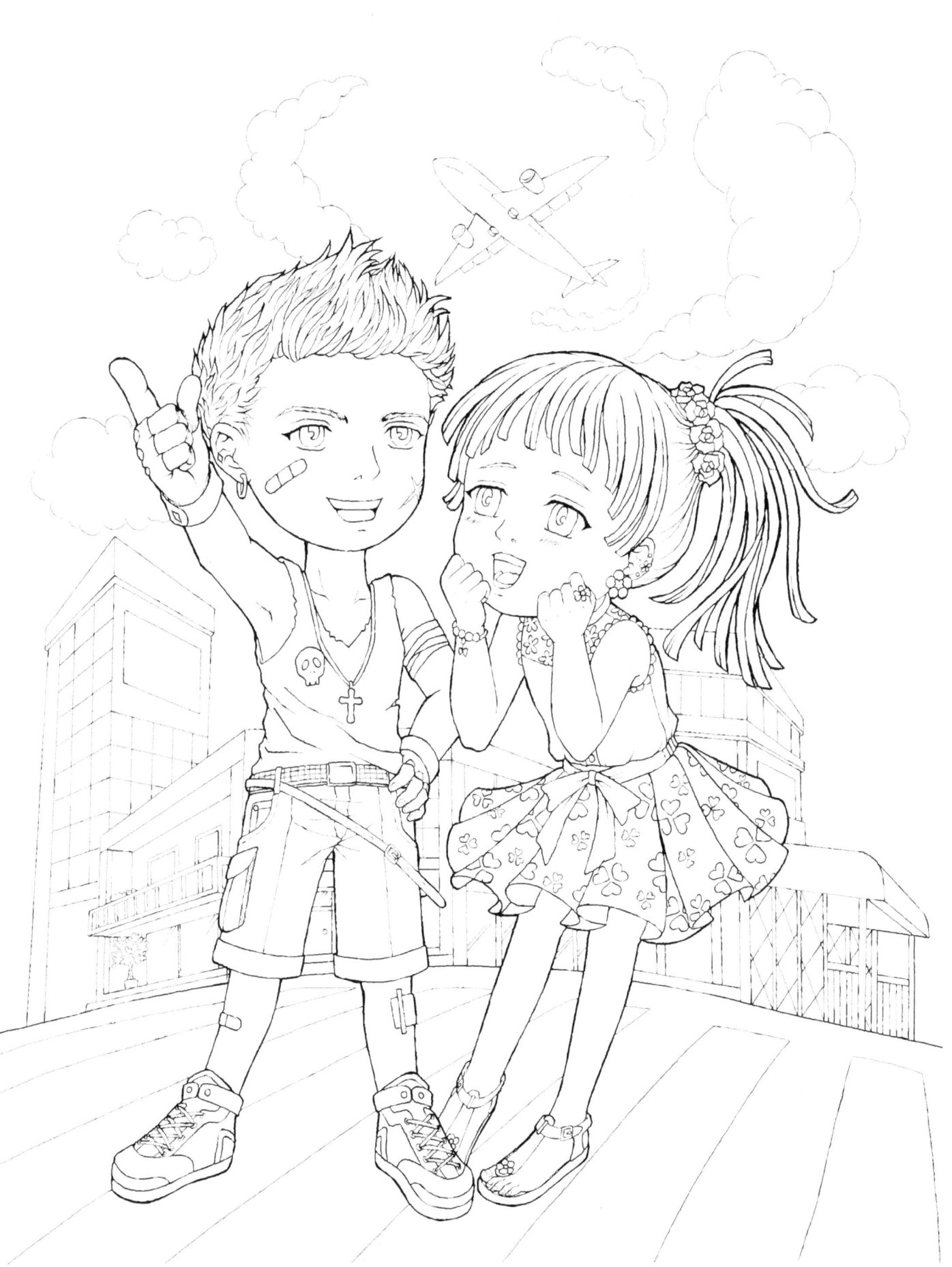

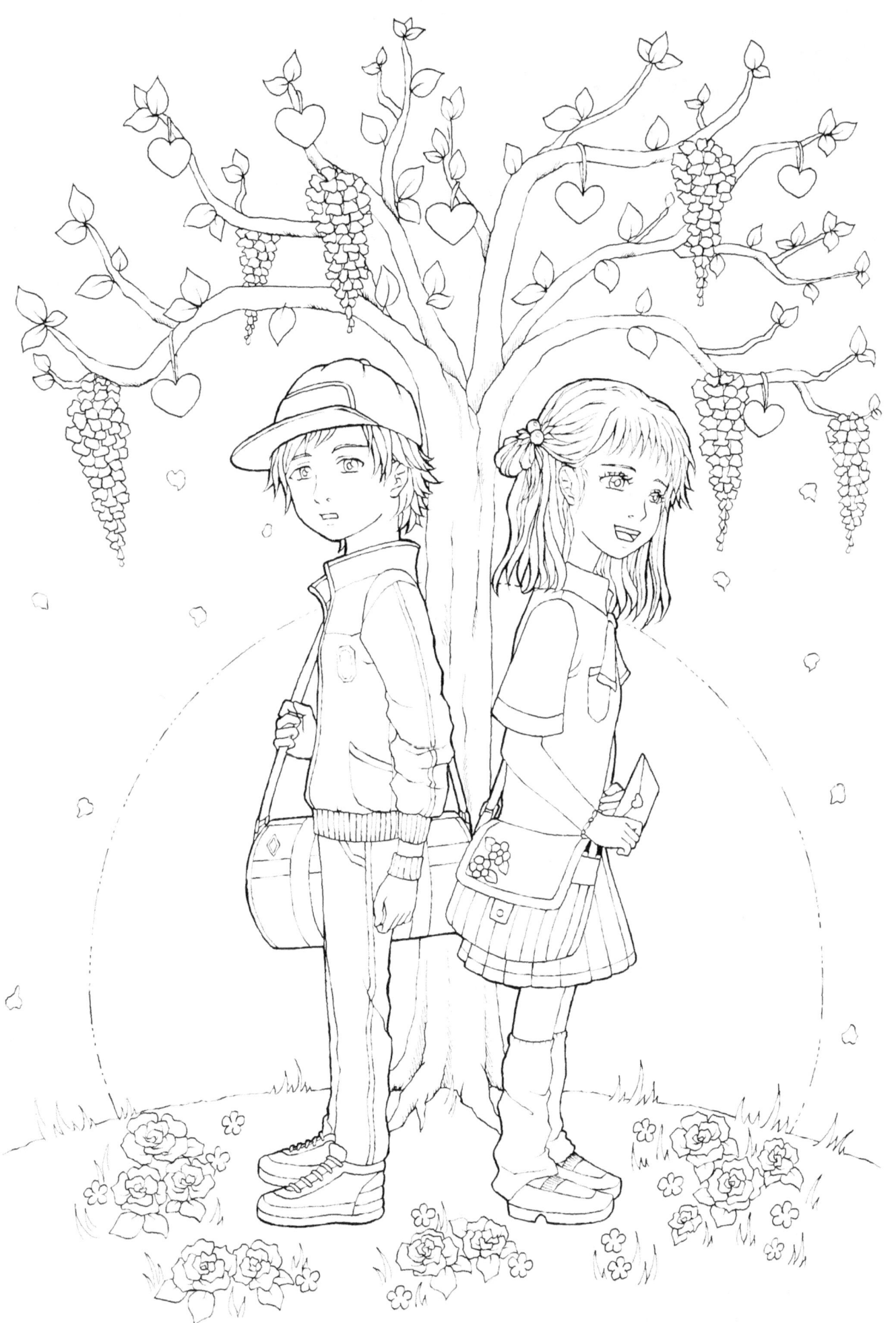

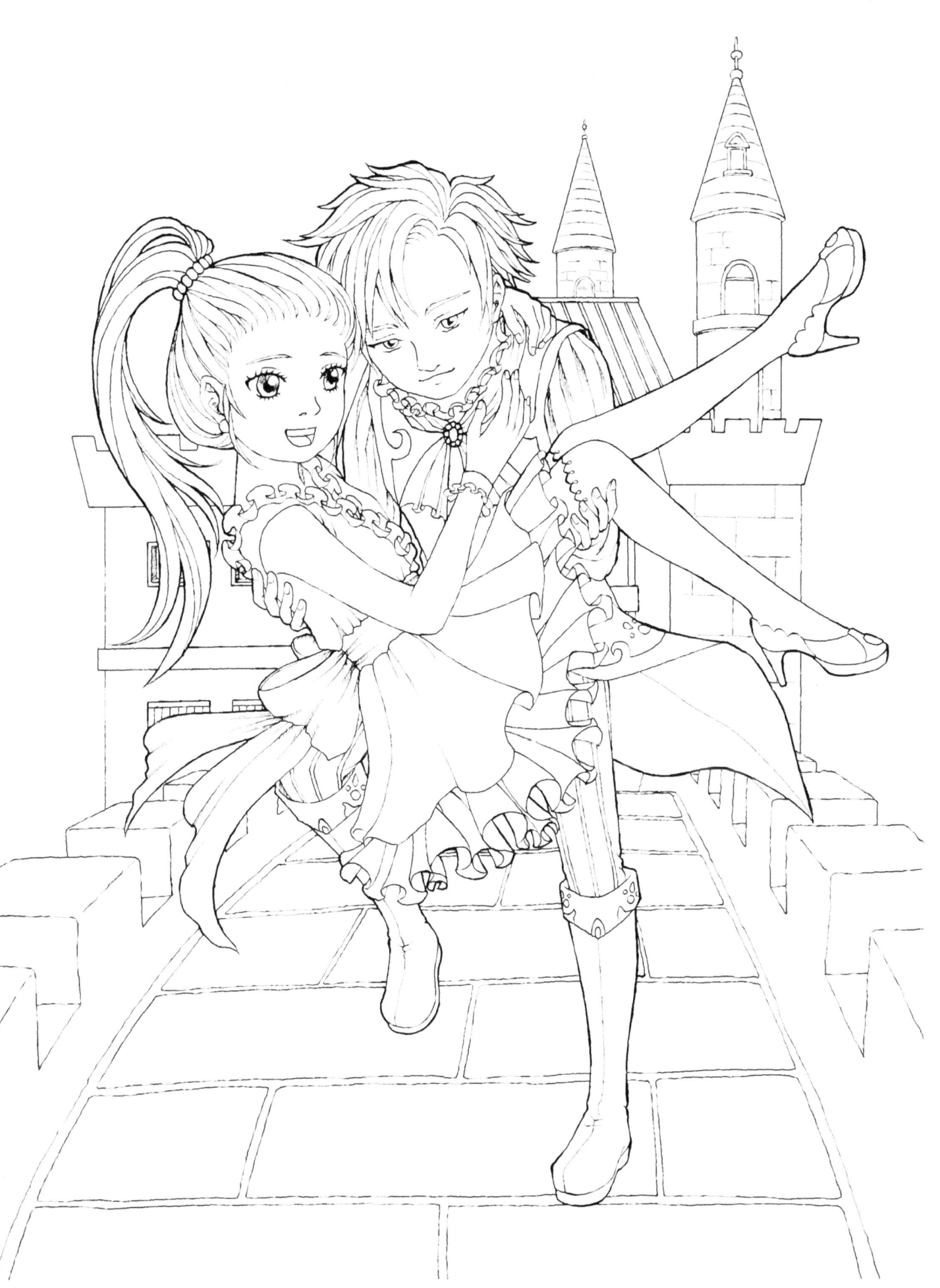

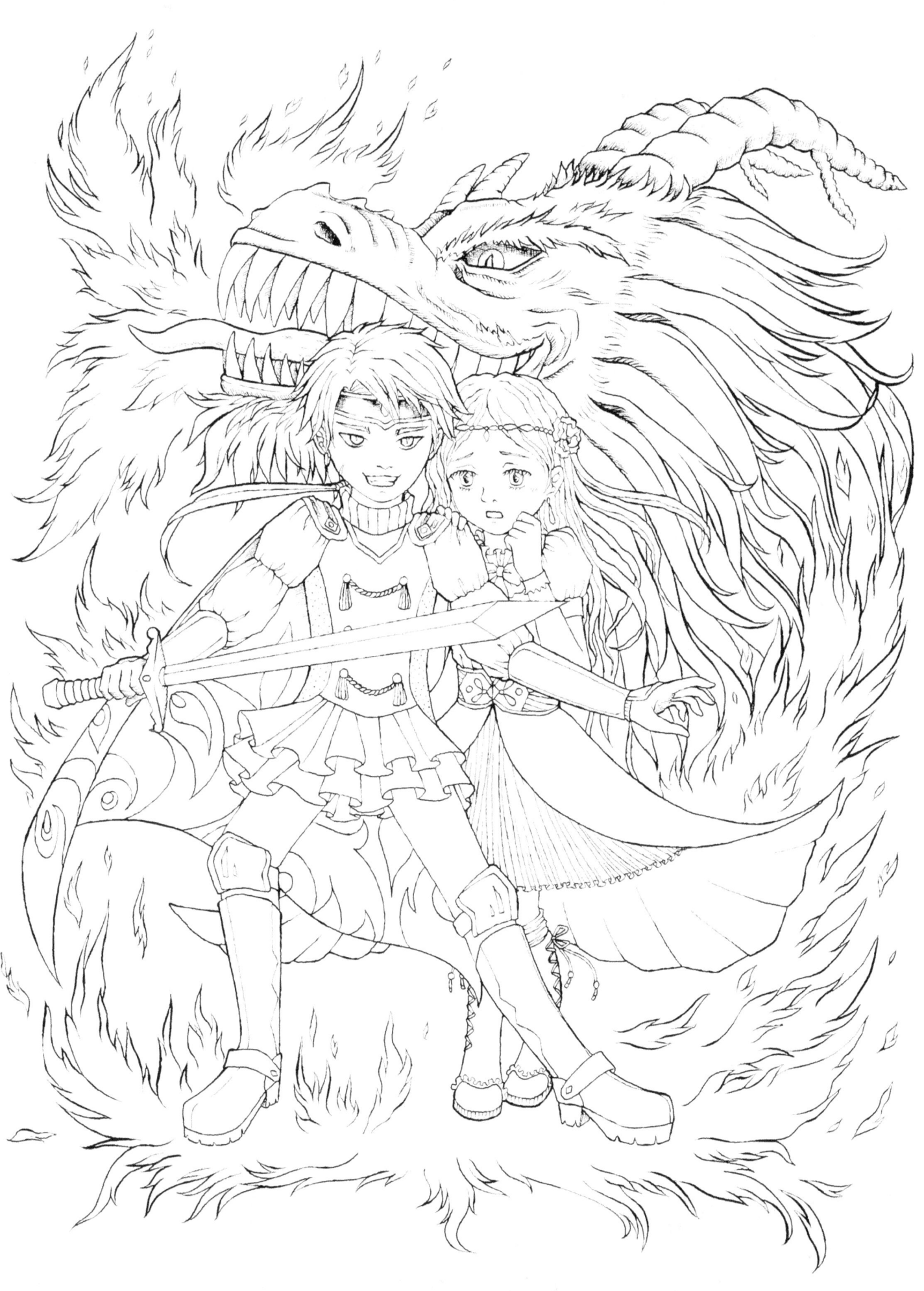

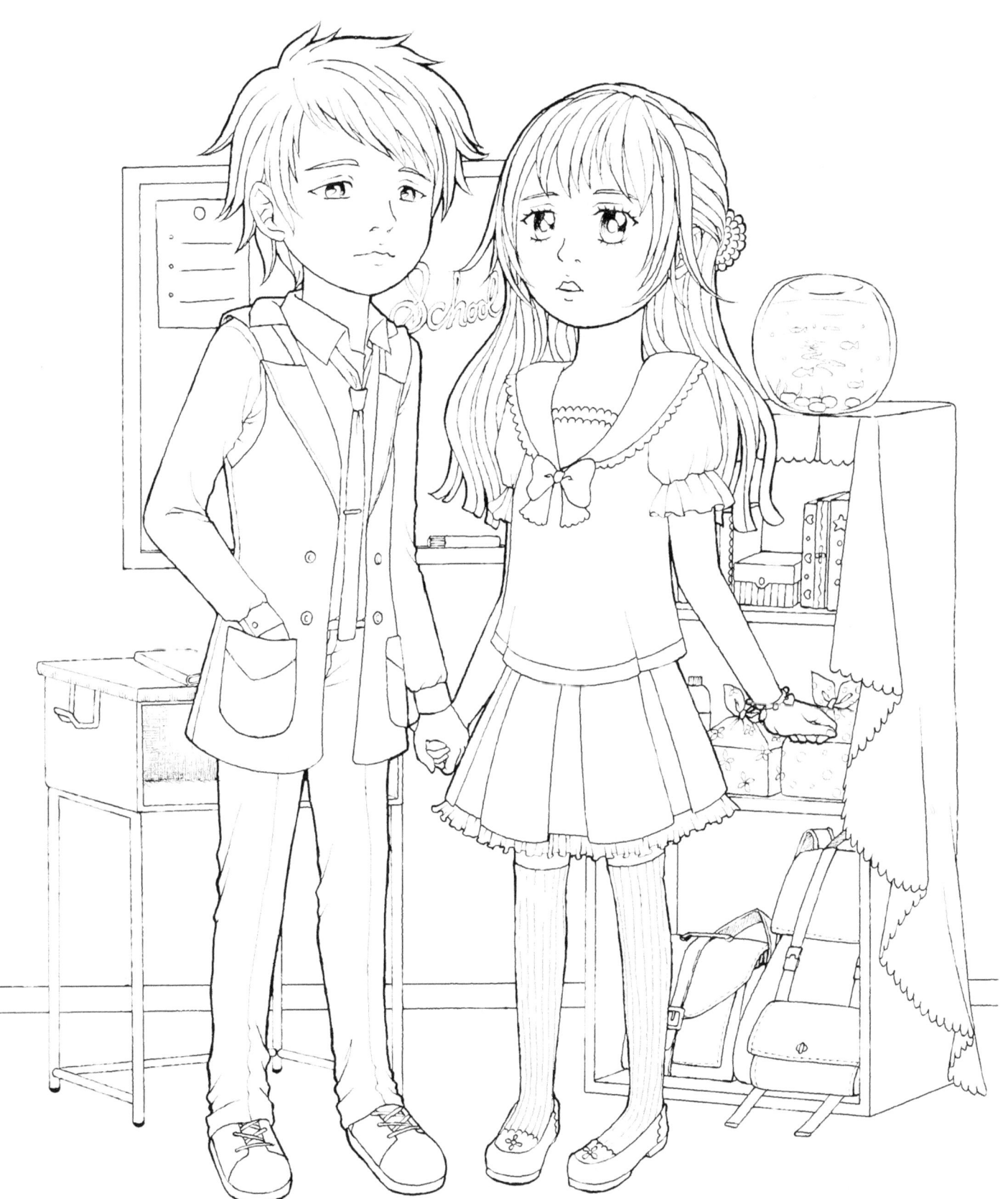

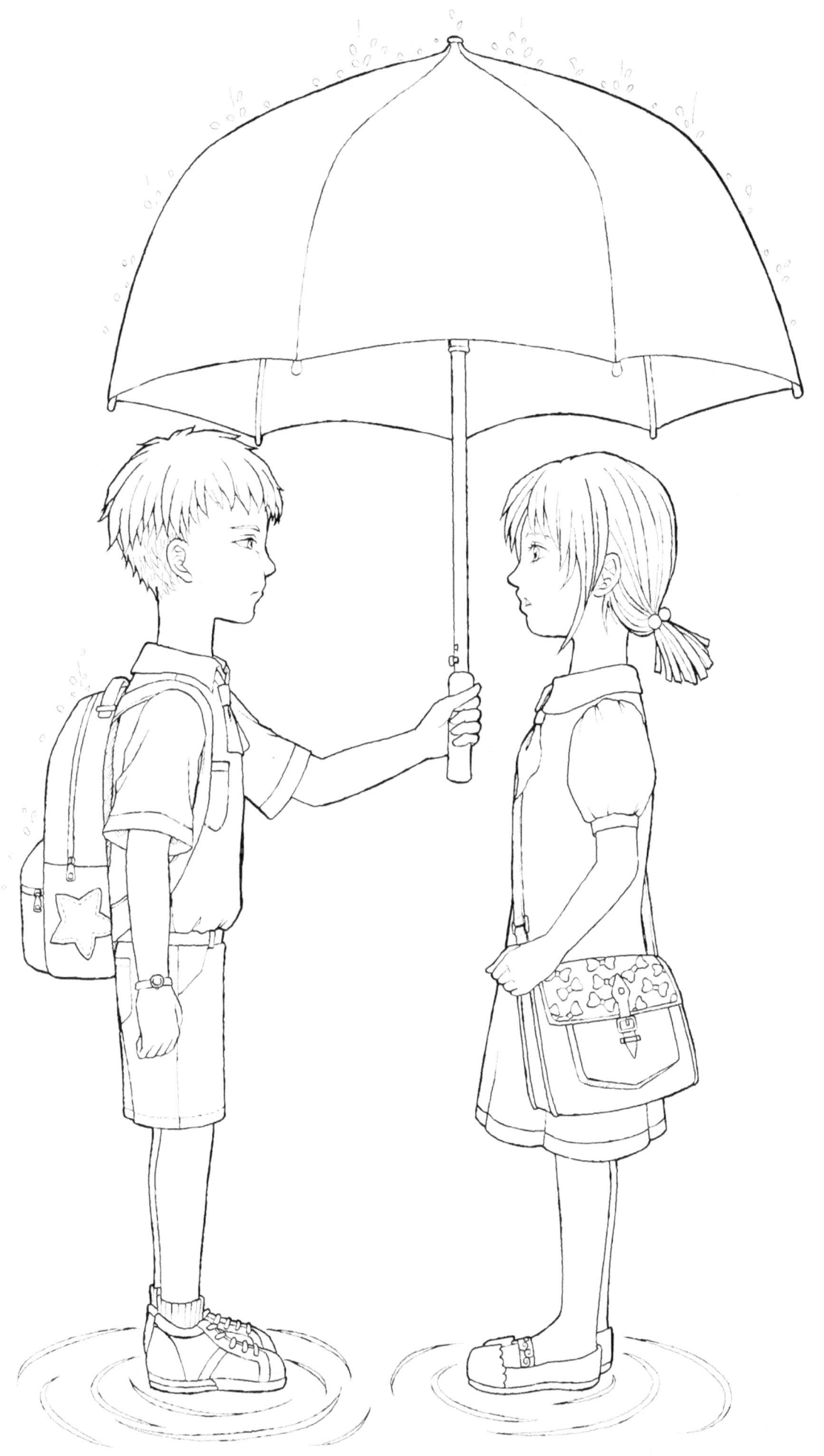